# BACK ROADS
### *of My*
# MEMORY

# BACK ROADS
## *of My*
# MEMORY

### Dr. Norman Hall
*with* Delores Hittinger

LifeRich
PUBLISHING

LifeRich Publishing is a registered trademark of The Reader's Digest Association, Inc.

LifeRich Publishing books may be ordered through booksellers or by contacting:

LifeRich Publishing
1663 Liberty Drive
Bloomington, IN 47403
www.liferichpublishing.com
1 (888) 238-8637

Because of the dynamic nature of the Internet, any web addresses or links contained in this book may have changed since publication and may no longer be valid. The views expressed in this work are solely those of the author and do not necessarily reflect the views of the publisher, and the publisher hereby disclaims any responsibility for them.

Any people depicted in stock imagery provided by Thinkstock are models, and such images are being used for illustrative purposes only. Certain stock imagery © Thinkstock.

ISBN: 978-1-4897-1498-5 (sc)
ISBN: 978-1-4897-1497-8 (hc)
ISBN: 978-1-4897-1499-2 (e)

Library of Congress Control Number: 2018902507

Print information available on the last page.

LifeRich Publishing rev. date: 3/23/2018

To

# *Billye Hall,*

my wife and best friend.

You inspired me
in all the accomplishments
of my lifetime.

You were the guiding spirit of our family.

# FOREWORD

EARLIER THIS YEAR, I INSISTED THAT DR. HALL document some of his life's stories because of all the years he has been an educator. I am impressed with his ability to begin as an educator in 1941 in a one-room schoolhouse to success in the Technology Age. I wanted him to share all his experiences, from sending students to the creek to get a bucket of drinking water for his students to the present day, when he is the superintendent of ten charter schools whose role is approving smart boards and all the other kinds of technology for the students of today.

His other stories document what it was like living in Texas for ninety-four years. As an educator myself, I am excited to share the book with others because it is rich in history.

—Delores Hittinger
retired educator

# CONTENTS

Introduction ............................................................ xvii

## PART I: MY BOYHOOD STORIES

A Bicycle with Pants on the Side of the Road .............. 3

The Midnight Ghost .................................................5

Raised with Mexican Children ...................................7

Mart Cox .................................................................9

A Rattle in the Dark................................................ 11

Passage by Cedar Limbs ......................................... 13

Saturday Trade Day................................................. 15

Setting the Car on Fire............................................ 17

Driven from the Profession...................................... 21

Tennis and the Twelve-inch Frying Pan ....................23

Jim Baker and the Mule ..........................................25

The Party Line.........................................................27

Baseball, Poor-boy Style..........................................29

Three Peach Trees ...................................................32

A Different Kind of Hurt ........................................33

The Seventeen Acres of Misery ...............................34

The Crash of the Cotton Market .............................37

Shooting Cattle at the ﬞ Ranch.............................39

A Neighbor to Remember ........................42

Leon Loreja ..............................44

The Lure of Sandy Soil ..........................47

Temple Airport Lights ...........................49

A Put-down to Last a Lifetime.........................51

Learning to Dance ...........................54

Still Wear My Coat .............................55

Fighting on the School Bus .........................56

I'll Wait for You ...........................57

Prophet or Lucky? ...........................59

Rattlesnake Inn ...........................61

Five Was Not Enough ...........................62

## Part II: College Stories

Freight Trains in My Life ...........................67

Selling the Milk Cows...........................72

Country Boy to the Library...........................76

Short-term Friends...........................79

The Speech Teacher ...........................83

A Mule in the Fourth-floor Shower ...........................86

What Might Have Been: The Story of the Brown Jug 89

The de Soto Rock ...........................92

An Eighteen-wheeler ...........................95

Career Choices ...................................................... 98

The Spirit by My Side ............................................ 100

Misspelling at a High Level ................................... 102

## PART III: MY FAMILY'S STORIES

The Ranch Brand .................................................. 107

Kinfolk.................................................................. 109

My Mother's Hands ............................................. 112

The Meaning of Halt............................................115

I Had the Right of Way.........................................117

Size 8½ D ............................................................119

The Vanishing Wife.............................................. 122

The Barn Dormitory ............................................ 125

The Red Boots...................................................... 127

Old Bus with a Message Board............................. 130

One Size May Fit Many ....................................... 132

"Still Trying to Get Even!" .................................. 134

Deer Hunting Exposed......................................... 136

The Lizard and Romance ..................................... 138

Telltale Grades .................................................... 140

Double Speeding.................................................. 141

A Plastic Paddle and the Waterfall...................... 143

Never Say Noah Again ......................................... 146

Learning to Spend Money ................................... 149

Footlockers to the Restroom ..................................151

Charlie and the Gym Wall ................................ 153

On My Knees in the Bar Ditch ............................155

A Beginning Rancher ...................................... 158

A Shoe in the Mud .......................................... 161

So Far Out .................................................... 163

Out the Door with My Hands Up ......................... 164

Most of It Was Your Fault ................................. 167

Unhand Me, You Brute ..................................... 168

Don't Forget Santa Claus .................................. 170

A Pessimistic Attitude ...................................... 171

Lost Speaker Fees ........................................... 172

Hometown Charm ............................................174

Gray Moss Inn ............................................... 176

A Lesson Too Late ........................................... 178

The Restroom at the Fire Station ........................ 180

The High Diving Board ..................................... 183

Five Dollars and Twenty-one Years Later ............... 185

Too Much Information ...................................... 187

Hit Him Again ............................................... 188

You Wouldn't Believe Me if I Told You ................... 190

Skipcha ....................................................... 193

Too Many Titles ............................................. 195

Floodwaters on Bear Creek ................................ 197

He Can't Come Right Now ..................................... 199

The Search Is Over ............................................200

## PART IV: PROFESSIONAL STORIES

How Easy It Seemed ............................................ 217

Baking on One Side while Freezing on the Other.... 219

Twenty-one Miles down the River ......................... 221

Paid by Voucher .................................................226

A Barber by Appointment ...................................228

Elsie .................................................................230

Shoot the Principal .............................................232

The Grade Book ................................................ 235

Trigger Gormley..................................................238

Identical Twins...................................................240

The Other Side of the Hill..................................242

How Do I Smell from Here? ...............................244

Uncontrolled Spending........................................246

Motivation at Its Lowest.....................................248

Sam Reid—A Lasting Impression..........................250

The Magic Basketball Court................................253

Searching for the Second-dumbest One in the Class 256

Didn't I Mention That to You? ...........................259

A Great Small Town...........................................262

Two Blankets under the Bridge ...........................264

The Lampasas Research Study ................................ 268

Paper Towels and Years Gone By ........................... 270

A Hole in a Shoe ................................................. 272

A Warning Too Late ............................................. 274

The Andrews School Board ................................... 277

The School Board Policy Handbook ....................... 280

The Question ...................................................... 282

An Extra Year of Development .............................. 284

Football—Rodeoing—Welding ............................. 286

No Driver's License Needed .................................. 289

Seventeen Touches .............................................. 292

My Most Creative Moment ................................... 294

A Multimillionaire without Milk ........................... 296

Twenty-seven Students ........................................ 299

Best-laid Plans ................................................... 302

No One Knows My Name ..................................... 305

Checking Speed with a Highway Patrolman ............ 307

No Ticket for Speeding at Your Age ...................... 310

A Delayed Hug ................................................... 312

Cardboard for Dinner .......................................... 313

Guilty: Not Recognizing Kids' Cries for Help .......... 315

## Part V: Things I Have Learned

As Time Goes By ...................................................... 319

Broken Futures.......................................................... 320

The Best Compliment I Ever Had .......................... 321

Prune Juice.............................................................. 322

A Referee Gone South ............................................ 324

Stealing Your Tomorrow.......................................... 325

Young People and the Elderly ................................. 326

Judging Character ................................................... 327

The Middle Age Test ............................................... 328

Food for Thought.................................................... 329

Fascination of an Attitude ....................................... 331

A Rule of Thumb to Live By.................................... 332

The Worst Thing about Growing Old...................... 333

## Part VI: Travel

The Switchblade ...................................................... 337

Inside the Cold War ................................................ 339

The Allenby Bridge.................................................. 341

Out to Sea in a Canoe .............................................343

## Part VII: Stories I Like to Tell

A Dog and Cat Story................................................349

Football Made Easy.................................................. 351

Small Things First .................................................. 354

Fishing with a Telephone Line.............................. 356

Light Humor....................................................... 358

The Curb.............................................................. 359

Property Ownership ............................................. 361

The Chimney and Indians.................................... 363

Easy-to-get-to Hip Pockets .................................. 365

Another Cat ......................................................... 367

A Cut-rate Donation............................................. 368

Rounding Up Cattle on a Motorcycle................... 370

Aggies' Kissing Tradition..................................... 372

Waiting on the Flower Seeds ................................ 374

Put the Hat Back On ........................................... 376

Can't Teach an Old Dog New Tricks ................... 378

He Walked Everywhere He Went.......................... 380

The Long Wait .................................................... 382

Exposed from a Camper........................................ 384

Traveling Interstate 10 by Flashlight.................... 386

# INTRODUCTION
## Back Roads of My Memory

From midnight to the hours of early dawn, my thoughts often wander to the back roads of my memory. I ponder the successes and failures of my life, the whys and the why-nots, the might-have-beens, the near-misses, and the what-ifs along with the forks in the road of life. I had been a country boy with limited success in the early years of my education. I entered college with what I feel was perhaps a fifth-grade reading level and very limited math skills.

I finished high school and received a bachelor's degree from Texas A&M, along with a commission in the US Army. I had limited ambition for my future until I spent four years in the army. During that time, I realized the need for a planned future. I readily admit that much of my success as an adult is due to the girl I married, Billye Barr. I loved her so much that I developed a constant desire to please her and make her proud of my accomplishments. She not only inspired me, she also raised our two fine sons almost by herself because I was often away working, attending professional workshops or seminars, and fulfilling speaking engagements.

I experienced a selfish childhood, which extended into my teen years. I never realized the sacrifices my mother and dad made to send me to college.

I was raised in a modest ranch home, but for Billye, I tried to build a mansion. I obtained the rank of major in the US Army Reserve and received a doctor of education degree from Colorado State College (now the University of Northern Colorado). I have never tired of learning, and, as an adult, I have always searched for something I did not know.

Billye and I traveled the world. On one occasion, we even went on a trip around the world. Over a period of forty years, we visited one hundred and six countries and returned to twenty-eight of them more than once! We often left the beaten "tourist's trails." We visited Vietnam and Outer Mongolia. We journeyed to Russia during the Cold War years. We went deep into China and explored the Great Wall. We even went beyond the Arctic Circle. We also went to Sweden, New Guinea, Cambodia, and Bora Bora.

After seventy-three years of married life, Billye passed

away at age eighty-nine. We had a wonderful life of love and respect. We enjoyed raising two fine sons. Billye and I lived a life of adventure and travel.

Several weeks after Billye's funeral, my sons and I ordered a grave marker to be placed in the cemetery at the gravesite. We went through the process of determining the name and age details for our shared gravestone. The last detail was the selection of the one line to go below the other details. We looked at a number of statements, trying to make a suitable selection. Finally, Charlie came up with a selection we all wholeheartedly agreed upon: "A True Love Story." The fact that my two sons came up with this selection meant so much to me. I had always thought ours was a storybook marriage, but for our two sons to think of it the same way gave me a remarkable sense of accomplishment. This acknowledgement from my sons was better than any compliment or award ever bestowed upon me.

In the coming pages, you will be exposed to a variety of my experiences, some 165, to be exact. These experiences cover more than the ninety-four years of my life. I have had a great life with many memories. At age ninety-four, I am thankful that I have the back roads of a lifetime of memories to travel and reflect upon.

# My Boyhood Stories

During the 1920s and 1930s, ranch life in the Hill Country of Texas was enjoyable, even though it was isolated and at times lonely. Our ranch was one of only two in a three-mile area. The roads were mainly dirt, and the rural mail carrier was our chief source of news. Even the newspaper was a day old when we received it. My life was made up of many carefree days experiencing ranch life and the small-town atmosphere. I graduated from Killeen High School in 1939 and entered college shortly thereafter.

*When I was in school during the twenties and thirties, the only terrorist we knew was the high school principal.*
– UNKNOWN

# A BICYCLE WITH PANTS ON THE SIDE OF THE ROAD

I HAD A BICYCLE I RODE UP AND DOWN THE COUNTRY road. The sides of this road were not mowed, and, in the spring, large blood weeds grew to as much as five or six feet high in the ditch on each side. When I was in grammar school, my favorite place to ride was down this country road about three hundred yards to a wooden bridge covering a small stream.

During the summer, my attire was usually very casual. I wore an old pair of jeans, no underwear, and no shirt. I usually rolled my pant leg up several times on the chain side of the bicycle to avoid getting it caught in the chain. When that did happen, the bike would come to an abrupt stop. This had happened to me several times, so I was not too worried because most of the time, I could free my pants from the chain without getting off the bicycle. But this time, the knot was so large that I had to get off and attempt to free the pant leg from the chain. Finally, it became necessary for me to take my pants off so I could work on freeing the leg.

Usually, few if any cars came along this isolated road, but that was not the case this day! At least four cars passed by within minutes of each other. Since I was without clothes, I retreated to the ditch beyond the blood weeds. I knew the people in each car that passed. They all stopped and viewed the bicycle with the pants still attached to the chain. They asked if they could help. I replied from behind the blood weeds, "No, thanks. I appreciate your offer to help." After the fourth car, I took the bicycle through the tall blood weeds into the ditch where I freed the knot from the bicycle and completed my trip to the bridge before returning home.

For months after this occasion, whenever I was in a group, Norman's bicycle-riding uniform was often a topic of discussion. I finally admitted to the event and laughed with the others.

*All progress takes place outside the comfort zone.*
– MICHAEL JOHN BOBAK

# THE MIDNIGHT GHOST

LIVING IN THE HILL COUNTRY NEAR KILLEEN, TEXAS, people had for years told a tale about a midnight ghost. I became curious about this ghost specifically when I was a teenager. A lady named Aunt Hull owned a ranch northwest of town. Rumor was that there was a certain spot on her ranch that on any date when there was a new moon, one could dig about three feet down to discover a large, flat rock about six feet long and three feet across. If you waited there until midnight, the image of a Mexican lady would appear and reveal directions to a place where silver bullion was hidden.

This fascinating story intrigued many teenagers who were looking for excitement, and I was certainly one of them. During my teenage years, on three different occasions, a group of us went to the spot and dug down to the flat rock. We planned to wait until midnight for the appearance of the ghost.

We did not ever stay until midnight. I think the closest we came was eleven forty, so I never did hear the directions to the silver stash.

*Defeat does not prevent final victory.*
– GEORGE W. BUSH

# RAISED WITH MEXICAN CHILDREN

My ranch life was combined with my life on a cotton plantation. My playmates were Mexican children because there were at least a dozen children from the Mexican families who lived on the ranch.

As we played together, I learned their language and many of their customs. I ate at their table and respected their parents. Then, when the Great Depression came in 1929, many of these families moved away. Years later, while serving in the army, a number of Mexicans were in my company. I enjoyed working with them and enjoyed being able to help with some of the language problems they encountered.

Still later, as I served as a school principal, Mexican children could attend public school. I still recall how in those early years the children seemed so alone and frightened in this new environment, so I tried to help them feel a part of the school. My childhood experiences on the ranch helped me relate to them and their situations.

Not until 1949 did the first Mexican student graduate from Killeen High School. I felt a sense of pride and accomplishment for them. I thought, *The Mexican race is on its way to equality.* Today, at the age of ninety-four, I realize that some of my best friends and associates have been Mexicans. My respect and admiration for the Mexican race and culture was developed in my character as I grew up on the ranch in the 1920s. I have never lost my fondness for my playmates of years past.

*In America, our origins matter less than our destination.*
– RONALD REAGAN

# MART COX

MART COX WAS A BLACKSMITH IN KILLEEN, TEXAS, during the 1920s, '30s, and '40s. His blacksmith shop was located within the city limits on a dirt road in a really large shed made from tin sheets that were nailed together.

One time, Mart's granddaughter had a seed wart growing on her index finger. Mart had a bottle of some kind of yellow liquid that he applied directly to her wart with a matchstick. After several applications, the wart went away.

The granddaughter shared this information with her friends at school. Soon, students began going to Mart's shop during the noon hour and after school to request the treatment for their warts. Amazingly, all the treatments were successful.

My information about the treatment for warts is firsthand because I was one of the kids waiting in line. This happened in the late 1930s. One can only imagine the severity of the punishment this good-natured man would suffer today for using such a treatment even though he was not charging for it. He only felt he was doing a community service.

*During the 1930s, the town where I lived had two fine doctors. They did not believe in needless surgery. If they did not need the money, they would not operate. However, there was not a person within a ten-mile radius of our town who still had a gallbladder.*
– UNKNOWN

# A RATTLE IN THE DARK

RANCH LIFE COULD BE SOMEWHAT PRIMITIVE DURING the 1920s and 1930s. There was no electricity, and few homes had water piped into their kitchens. This was also before air conditioning, so my main priority in life was being comfortable. It was the custom for many rural people to prepare a bed in the yard to take advantage of any breeze that might be blowing.

In following this custom, I persuaded my dad to prepare a bed for us to sleep on outside one summer. Everything went well until a night in August when we were awakened by the barking of dogs and a loud rattle. We immediately recognized the rattle as that of a rattlesnake.

The dilemma we faced was frightening. Dad and I were in the bed in the yard without a light to find the snake, and there was a real danger in getting off the bed to find it because we could have stepped on it. Finally, Mother heard all the commotion and lit a kerosene lamp. The lamp provided Dad with enough light to race into the house to retrieve his shotgun. With the shotgun in hand and the glow from the kerosene lamp, he was able to find and kill the snake.

After all the drama ended, Dad said the snake was evidently crawling through our yard looking for water when the dogs became aware of his presence and began barking.

This event dampened some of my enthusiasm for sleeping in the yard, so the next year, we moved the bed to the safety of the front porch.

*A man was heard to say he was going to move to Texas as soon as he found out how far it is to "down yonder."*
– UNKNOWN

# PASSAGE BY CEDAR LIMBS

There were times when the weather conditions emphasized our isolation in the country. It was extremely difficult to travel into town, especially after a big rain. Our ranch was on a gravel road except for the last mile, which was only black gumbo dirt. When it rained two inches or more, the road was almost impassable by car.

One time, it had rained for several days, dropping around four inches. Our ranch and a neighbor's ranch were running out of supplies, so we decided that a trip to town must be made.

The plan was that Dad and the neighbor would cut limbs from the large cedar trees and place them in the deep ruts in the road. Then Mother was to drive the Model-T Ford down the ruts until she reached the gravel road. The progress was slow, but we made it to town and back.

I was only four years old when I witnessed this ingenious episode—from the front seat of the 1924 Model-T Ford.

*Individuals take different roads seeking fulfillment and happiness. Just because they are not on your road does not mean they have gotten lost.*
– H. JACKSON BROWN, JR.

# SATURDAY TRADE DAY

During the 1930s, the merchants of Killeen devised a plan to attract more shoppers to the community on the weekends. They decided to give numbered tickets to each person who purchased five dollars' worth of merchandise from the local stores. Each Saturday afternoon around three o'clock, a drawing was conducted, but the person with the winning ticket had to be present to win.

Preparations for the drawing were rather extensive. A fifteen-by-fifteen-foot platform about six feet high to be used for the drawing presentation was built at one of the two crossroads within the city limits.

One Saturday, the number on my ticket was drawn, and my prize was an electric clock. I was told the value of the clock was $7.50, which in 1930 was a tidy sum of money.

My enthusiasm was short-lived when I realized that I lived four miles out in the country with no electricity. I also understood that there was a limit to the length of an extension cord. On second thought, I realized that $7.50 in cash would not be unwelcome. The clock had been donated by Hubby's Jewelry Store, so I went there to talk to the jeweler about not being able to use the clock. After my explanation, he went directly to the cash register and took out one dollar and a half and placed it on the counter. I suppose my expression of disappointment and disbelief prompted his explanation. He told me that while the selling price of the clock was advertised as $7.50 during the Saturday Trade Day, the wholesale cost of the clock was the only amount qualifying for a refund.

On that day, this twelve-year-old boy lost part of his dream of fair play in the American economic system.

*A nickel ain't worth a dime anymore.*
– YOGI BERRA

# SETTING THE CAR ON FIRE

NOWADAYS, FEW PEOPLE REMEMBER THE OLD MODEL-T Ford. It was black, of course, with a front and back seat. There was no door on the driver's side, and I always wondered why.

The car was open, and the only glass was the windshield. In the winter, black curtains were put up all around the car. Each curtain had a one-foot square cut in it, and isenglass was sewed into the curtain to provide visibility to the outside. In many cases, after a period, the isenglass would break, leaving gaped edges. This situation presented no physical danger as the isenglass would break easily.

One day, when I was about twelve or thirteen years old, I was standing by our Model-T with my friend, J. L. Williams. We were waiting for my mother to come from the house to go and deliver eggs and butter to some merchants in Killeen. I had read somewhere that a certain type of isenglass would not burn. I announced this bit of information to J. L., who immediately contested my assertion.

Since our car had part of the isenglass broken off, I decided to prove I was right by lighting a match and holding it up to the broken window in the curtain. The glass blazed into a quick flame, which immediately spread to the curtain. In a matter of only a few seconds, the curtain was consumed with fire which quickly spread to the canvas car top.

At this point, while I was trying to beat the fire out with my hand, I shouted at J. L. to get a bucket of water. I desperately began throwing sand from the driveway onto the burning areas, and burning pieces of the top began to fall on the back seat which immediately caught fire!

Finally, J. L. returned with a large bucket of water to throw on the fire. It was eventually fully extinguished, but not before the car suffered extensive damage. Half of the top was burned, as well as several of the curtains and some of the back seat.

Shortly after we had the fire put out, my mother came out the door of our house. When she stepped onto the porch, which was about three feet higher than the car, she screamed and dropped the basket of eggs and the butter. She shouted, "What happened to my car?"

I provided her with an explanation about the article I had read and what had caused the fire. She did not seem to be paying any attention. She got into the car and started the motor without another word. Quickly, J. L. and I climbed in and endured dead silence all the way to town.

Since J. L. lived in town, he eagerly asked to be dropped off before we delivered the eggs and butter. This left me a very abandoned and lonely passenger in the car.

As a rule, Mother parked her car in the back of the store when making a delivery. But this time she drove down the long block in front of the store, made a turn at the end of the block, and parked directly in front of the store.

By the time Mother parked the car, many of the farmers and ranchers who were in town for Saturday shopping had gathered on the sidewalk and were looking at Mother's car. I felt about two feet tall as I sat there waiting for Mother to exit. As she stepped onto the sidewalk, several people asked, "Lola, what happened to your car?"

Her reply? "Norman set it on fire." And with that, she entered the store.

My only punishment for my behavior was how matter-of-factly my mother responded to the people about the damage to her car as if this act were to be expected from me. I am now over ninety years old, and I still can hear my mother's scream when she saw the car.

*It is easier to ask for forgiveness than it is to ask permission.*
– UNKNOWN

# DRIVEN FROM THE PROFESSION

WHEN I WAS IN EIGHTH GRADE, MY MOTHER NOTICED IN our local weekly paper that free guitar lessons were available to interested individuals. Upon further investigation, it was determined that the lessons were designed for a steel guitar.

Mother thought this was an opportunity to bring out any hidden musical talent that might be lurking somewhere in my inner self. At any rate, we purchased a guitar and other materials and equipment necessary to launch my musical career.

Lessons were scheduled once a week for five weeks, which supposedly provided ample time for practice. Practice was fun, at first, but soon, practice turned into forced time on task. As I slid the steel bar up and down the strings at each lesson, I could see the instructor cringe and squirm in his chair. Each of my lessons ended with an evaluation of my progress, and every evaluation included a rather strong comment that I was not practicing nearly enough.

At the end of the five free lessons, my mother thought we should continue with paid lessons. I was not in favor of this extension of my lessons; however, the issue never came up for a vote.

The day arrived when we were to inform the instructor of the decision to continue my lessons. When we arrived at his studio, the instructor was not there, but his wife was and informed us that he had given up on providing lessons due to the lack of progress of a number of his students. He had now decided to take a job as a carpenter.

I assumed I had driven him from his chosen profession.

*Failure is not necessarily a bad thing; it*
*could be an opportunity to learn.*
– UNKNOWN

# TENNIS AND THE TWELVE-INCH FRYING PAN

During the late 1930s, I attended high school in Killeen, Texas, a small ranching and farming community. The total enrollment of the entire school system was around 325 students. The only outside activity for the younger students was the children's playground equipment that consisted of a slide, seesaws, and swings.

High school activities were limited to a blacktop tennis court, but only a few of the students had tennis rackets. Over a period of time, it became common practice to lend your racket to a bystander when you lost the game. The problem that arose here was the owner of the racket might lose the first game and never get to play again during the one-hour lunch period. So, the owners of the rackets decided not to lend their rackets to bystanders. This came as quite a shock to several students, especially for an individual who lived next door to the school grounds. When he was refused the use of the racket, he rushed home, secured a twelve-inch frying pan, and returned to the tennis courts. His desire to play with the pan caused quite a bit of controversy, but he was allowed to play. He was very good at playing net in a doubles match. As other frying pans began to appear at a rate of one a day, pans were finally forbidden. Once again, the games returned to the normal routine with the prescribed equipment.

*The attitude of the individual determines the attitude of the group.*
– JOHN MAXWELL

# JIM BAKER AND THE MULE

DURING THE 1920S AND 1930S, KILLEEN WAS A SMALL ranching and farming community in central Texas. Cattle, sheep, and goats provided the livelihood for most, as did a small amount of farming.

The community operated without a licensed veterinarian, but there was one person here who had some training and a wealth of experience in dealing with livestock. His name was Jim Baker, and he resided within Killeen. It had been common practice for a number of years that when any livestock had any kind of disease, Jim Baker was the first to be consulted.

Once, my father had a team of mules harnessed to distribute hay to a group of cattle. On the way to the feeding grounds, the team, wagon, and load of hay were driven through a gate. When my father stopped to close the gate, the mules were left standing in tall grass. A rattlesnake bit one of the mules on the front leg, and this was normally a slow form of death. Because mules were very valuable, steps had to be taken to save the mule if at all possible.

Jim Baker was called, and upon examination of the mule, he asked for two gallons of warm, sweet milk. He further stipulated that the milk must be fresh from the cow. After the milk cans were located and filled with fresh milk, Jim took the mule's leg, lifted it up, and placed it in the can of milk so that the milk covered the snakebite. He prescribed that the milk needed to be changed again every two hours for at least six hours.

The mule recovered, and in about three weeks, he took his regular turn in the ranch operations. I had not heard of this treatment before, and I have not heard of it since—but it worked!

*A mind once stretched by a new idea never*
*regains its original dimensions.*
– OLIVER WENDELL HOLMES

# THE PARTY LINE

FROM THE 1920S THROUGH THE 1940S, THE PHONE company installed one telephone line that was shared among many people. This was called a party line. There were times when as many as eight people would share the same telephone line. When a call was made, the phone rang in the homes of all the line members. To make a call, one would take the receiver from the hook and turn the handle of a crank-type instrument. A complete turn of the crank was called long, and a half turn was called short. For example, the sequence for our ranch was two long rings and one short ring.

The problem with this system was that everyone on the line knew when anyone was receiving a call. Many times, this resulted in several parties listening in on the conversations. At one time, two members of our party line were elderly ladies who spent most of the day and part of the night "tuning in" to conversations. It was not unusual for one of the ladies to interrupt by saying, "What did they say? I missed the last part of the sentence."

When I was in college in the early 1940s, I would call home fairly often. It was not uncommon for a member of the party line to jump into the conversation by asking a question or making a comment. The interruptions were bothersome, but we tried to look at the comical side and accept it as a way of life and a sign of the times.

*A teacher once made fun of my ability to help another student.*
*I never hated the man. I hated what the man*
*did to me in front of my classmates.*
*I am ninety-four years of age now, and I*
*have never forgotten the incident.*
– NORMAN HALL

# BASEBALL, POOR-BOY STYLE

DURING THE 1930S, BASEBALL WAS A BIG PART OF A boy's life. There was no broadcast of games, and the only source of information was the next day's newspaper with an account of the games played the previous day.

Our closest neighbor lived two miles away through what we called "the thicket," an area that was covered with trees and heavy brush, with only a narrow trail winding through it. The neighbor had two boys near my age, and during summer on Sunday afternoons, we occasionally went into Killeen to watch the grown men play baseball. There we saw real baseball. Seeing the gloves and the hats used in a real baseball game provided topics of conversation among us for days on end.

Even though we did not have a ball, a glove, or a bat, the urge to play the game was so strong that we would often improvise. Our garage door stayed closed most of the time, and it provided an excellent backstop. The end of a wooden apple box served as a base. We backed off some fifty feet and dug a hole to stand in as the pitcher's mound. For the bat, we removed one of the pickets from our yard fence. It was probably an inch and a half square and thirty-six inches long. For a ball, we used rocks about the size of a baseball. With this arrangement, we did not need a catcher or a fielder, just a pitcher and a batter. The skill of the pitcher determined the amount of practice the batter might get in backing away from the pitch or even ducking from a pitch that was inside the home plate.

The three of us did not know we were poor, so we enjoyed our poor-boy brand of baseball. In due time, a ball and bat came our way, but it took longer for us to acquire gloves. Later on, we built a wire backstop in the pasture and placed large rocks around for the bases. We even added a single fielder, while the backstop served as the catcher.

This activity served as a source of constant pleasure for the three of us. I have cherished these memories of poor-boy baseball for over seventy years. Incidentally, the youngest of the three of us went on to play on the University of Texas baseball team in Austin during the early 1940s.

*Success is the sum of small efforts repeated day in and day out.*
– ROBERT COLLIER

# THREE PEACH TREES

FAMILY LIFE IS MADE UP OF MANY MINUTE EVENTS THAT last a lifetime. The details of one such event follow.

Three peach trees grew outside our kitchen window, but they never produced peaches until I went away to college.

My mother and father had never heard of Dr. Benjamin Spock. Even if they had, it would not have made a difference. They firmly believed that if you "spared the rod, you spoiled the child." Thus, a very convenient way to administer corporal punishment was to jerk a limb off the peach trees and start the process immediately.

I haven't liked peaches since my childhood.

*There is a difference in the people who make a difference.*
– NORMAN HALL

# A DIFFERENT KIND OF HURT

When I was growing up on the ranch near Killeen, we knew we were poor people, but we locked the house when we left anyway. On one occasion, we were gone overnight. When we returned, it was obvious that someone had forced their way into the house. However, upon close examination, we could not find anything missing.

Can you imagine telling someone your house was broken into but nothing was taken? This was a different kind of hurt, but a real one. We knew we were poor, but we didn't know we were *that* poor.

*It takes confidence to dream big.*
– UNKNOWN

# THE SEVENTEEN
# ACRES OF MISERY

WE CALLED THE PLANT *MAIZE*. IT WAS A MEMBER OF THE sorghum family that we used as feed for the livestock. It grew some four feet high and produced a head of grain on top of the plant.

During my childhood, there were no combines or any type of machinery to harvest the heads of grain. The harvesting had to be done by hand in what seemed like a crude method, even back then. Someone armed with a large knife—in my case, me with a butcher's knife from my mother's kitchen—walked between the rows of sorghum. With one hand, I would grab the head of the grain. With the other hand, I made a slashing motion to separate the heads of grain from the stock of sorghum. The heads were placed in piles between the rows. I had no gloves, so by noon of the first day of harvest, a blister would form on the hand I used to hold the knife. This procedure continued all day or at least until just before the sun went down. Then to end the day's work, we took toe sacks and went down each row, sacking the maize heads. We had to be cautious when picking up these heads because rattlesnakes and copperhead snakes would crawl under them for shelter from the heat.

My dad usually planted three acres of maize each year, and it took a minimum of three days for us to harvest it all. Many times, after we completed the harvest, my dad would send me to a neighbor's farm to help them harvest their crop of maize. Needless to say, I hated the season when we harvested maize.

At the time, I really did not want to go to college, but to please my mother, I went. I endured it for a year. By the end of that first year, I had made my mind up that I was not going to return for the second year, so I packed my footlocker with all my possessions and headed home.

By late May or early June, the crops were almost ready to harvest. There was a winding gravel road that led past our farm, but before arriving at our farm, it topped a hill. From here, we enjoyed a panoramic view of the surrounding farmland. When I arrived at this point, I could see the three-acre field, and, of course, it was planted in maize. But that day, I was shocked and surprised to see that my dad had also planted another nearby fourteen-acre field in maize.

That sight of seventeen acres of maize changed my life's plan. I could not face seventeen acres of maize with a butcher knife. I could not endure all the blisters I would have. I could not deal with seventeen acres of sacking grain heads from piles that might have snakes under them.

In a period of less than ten minutes, my life's plan was changed forever. When I arrived home, I greeted my parents and announced that I could only stay the weekend because I wanted to attend summer school which started the next week.

Those seventeen acres taught me a profound lesson about life. I then spent seven years in college. I received a bachelor's degree, a master's degree, and a doctor's degree.

*If you don't know where you are going, you might wind up somewhere else.*
– YOGI BERRA

# THE CRASH OF THE
# COTTON MARKET

I WAS BORN IN 1922 AND RAISED ON A COMBINATION ranch and cotton farm. Our rural operation was based on a thousand-acre ranch where we raised cattle, sheep, and goats. My dad had 110 acres of this land under cultivation and leased some 300 additional acres from nearby neighbors.

During 1928, my father produced forty-eight bales of cotton. The selling price had reached forty-eight cents per pound, but Dad did not sell at that low price. He had the ginned bales delivered to the ranch because his goal was to sell at fifty cents per pound.

The beginning of the economic crash came on October 29, 1929. The price of cotton plunged from a high of forty-eight cents a pound to three cents a pound in a matter of days. My dad eventually sold all forty-eight bales for three cents a pound. He never fully recovered from the financial loss, and he blamed himself for poor management. Our way of life changed to a marked degree from that day on.

*Some of the people in my hometown joined welfare. We called them social climbers.*
– UNKNOWN

# SHOOTING CATTLE
# AT THE JJ RANCH

DURING THE DARK DAYS OF THE GREAT DEPRESSION
from 1929 to 1935, one of the concerns of the powers
that be was, of all the things, overproduction. This was
especially true of cotton and livestock. The overproduction
translated into low prices, even if a buyer could be found.

One of the solutions for overproduction was to plow
up the cotton plants in the fields before they produced
the bolls of cotton. Another was to take the livestock off
to market – killing the cattle, sheep, or goats, and not
permitting the meat products to be sold.

Our ranch was four miles northeast of Killeen, Texas,
and served as the assembly point for any rancher in the area
who wanted to take advantage of a government-created
market. Little did Dad realize what the designation as an
assembly point meant when he accepted the government's
offer to provide his ranch as the assembly point for our
area. My father lined 106 head of cattle up against a rail

fence at the ranch. Three government officials appeared to do the government's business. One quoted a price for each animal. The other had a .22-caliber rifle and the other, a clipboard. As the buyers moved down the line of cattle, the lead buyer would offer a price. The standard price was three dollars for each range animal and six dollars for the dairy cattle, no more and no less. If the rancher accepted the price, the man with the .22 rifle shot the animal between the eyes right in its tracks. The buyer moved on down the line, repeating this process.

Within an hour, 106 animals lay dead along the fence. Three cowboys were employed to drag the bodies to a ravine on our ranch property. One cannot imagine what it looks like to see 106 dead animals stacked in a ravine. The law stated that no part of the animal could be sold – it all had to be destroyed. My father was given fifteen gallons of gasoline to be used in burning this pile of animals. The problem was that raw meat does not readily burn, and the stench persisted for several days.

This method of fighting the Great Depression was viewed as woeful waste since people were starving throughout the land. But the hard fact was that the money paid was more than the ranchers could receive elsewhere. The meager amount of cash received was, in most cases, an aid in surviving the agony of the times.

For me, a nine-year-old boy, this event left a lasting impression that still haunts me.

*The government can't give to anybody anything that the government doesn't first take from somebody else.*
– IVAN DUNCAN

# A NEIGHBOR TO REMEMBER

IN 1918, A FLU EPIDEMIC SPREAD THROUGHOUT MOST OF the United States. The epidemic had much to do in changing the lives of my mother and her two children. Mother had first married a farmer, to whom two sons were born. During the summer of 1918, her husband contracted the flu. It hit hard and confined him to bed for a period of three weeks before he died.

The flu was so contagious that people refused to come in contact in any way with people who were exposed. Mother's farm was located seven miles from Killeen. A brother-in-law, the president of the local bank, rode his horse out to the farm every few days to bring groceries and medical supplies. He never came into the house. He placed what he brought at the yard gate. He would exchange a few words with Mother and return to town.

On the next farm less than a mile away, lived Mike Cook, a farmer who was married with six children. During the time of Mother's husband's illness, Mike came every day to help Mother bathe her husband and do the necessary chores about the farmhouse.

Mike Cook did this service even though he knew how contagious the flu could be. He never seemed to consider that he might contract the disease or how it could affect his family.

Years later, Mother married my father. I came along two years later. Often during my childhood, I heard my mother refer to Mike Cook. She always recalled with deep gratitude his service and sacrifices during her family's time of need.

*At nighttime, throw one of your shoes under*
*the bed just as far as you can.*
*Why? Because the next morning, you start the day on your knees.*
– UNKNOWN

# LEON LOREJA

During my childhood years, I knew nothing about discrimination. I lived on a ranch where I laughed and played with eleven Mexican children who were within three to four years of my age.

Three Mexican families lived and worked on our ranch. All the family members spoke Spanish; few spoke any English. Naturally, with them speaking Spanish, I learned to speak their language. My dad and I often spoke Spanish at the dinner table, against the wishes of my mother. She often said, "When Norman starts school, his speaking Spanish will handicap him."

Also living on the ranch was an elderly Mexican gentleman by the name of Leon Loreja. My dad had been his friend for a number of years. Dad had given Leon three acres of land on which he built a one-room log cabin, cultivated the land, built a corral, and developed a yard area around his cabin. Over a period of time, he acquired three horses, two goats, and a number of chickens. He was a self-sufficient man.

Leon often ate with us at the same table. To us, this was normal, but I learned of the amazement of our Anglo neighbors at such behavior. My dad trusted Leon, and he gave him many responsibilities around the ranch.

The day came when Leon told us that he would be leaving the ranch. He wanted to die among his own family in Mexico. I recall the emotional scene at the bus station when Mother, Dad, and I took him to catch the bus for his Mexican destination.

During the next several months, we received two letters from Leon. The writing was in "Tex-Mex," which we could not make out. My mother took each letter to the high school Spanish teacher for help interpreting the content, but she was also unable to interpret it.

Leon disappeared from our presence, but we never forgot him. I played in and around his log cabin for a number of years, and I have fond memories of his time at the ranch.

Note: Mother was right! The summer before I started school, she sent me to town to live with an aunt who was an English teacher at the local high school. She was told to help me learn to speak proper English.

*There is no road like the road back home.*

– UNKNOWN

# THE LURE OF SANDY SOIL

DURING MY CHILDHOOD YEARS, WE LIVED IN AN AREA of central Texas where the soil was black and muddy. Ranching and farming was a hard way to make a living. My mother had a sister who lived in west Texas on a sandy-soil farm. Their farm received adequate rainfall each year, so it produced good crops without fail.

From time to time, the two sisters discussed how nice it would be if we sold our ranch and moved to west Texas and started a farm. One farm that was near my aunt's place was recommended to my dad. Finally, he agreed to go to west Texas and look over the prospect of farming. Much to the disappointment of the sisters, after he made the trip to look at the farm, he decided not to move to west Texas.

A number of years later, I was living in Andrews, Texas, which is about thirty miles from Seagraves, where the farm of interest was located. To my surprise, there were nine producing oil wells on the property.

My mother and father were in their eighties by this time, so I never told them the truth about the lure of sandy soil that produces oil.

*The happiest people don't necessarily have the best of everything; they just make the best of what they have.*
– UNKNOWN

# TEMPLE AIRPORT LIGHTS

DURING MY HIGH SCHOOL DAYS, HUNTING AT NIGHT with dogs was a favorite pastime of country boys. There was no TV, and entertainment by radio was quite limited. We usually hunted on top of a range of hills we called mountains, north of Killeen. The mountains were covered with post oak timber that was so thick in places that you could not ride a horse through them.

We hunted for raccoons, foxes, and opossums. When sold, their hides provided us with spending money. For example, a raccoon hide would bring one dollar, a fox hide would bring about three dollars, and an opossum hide would bring at least thirty cents. This was not bad money in those days.

Occasionally, the mountains would be covered with low clouds, which restricted our visibility of the stars we relied on to help us find our direction. Once we knew where north was, we could find our way home. When the low clouds covered the stars, we resorted to another direction finder.

Temple, Texas, was twenty-five miles away. The only airport in what we called central Texas was there in Temple. It had a strong rotating light that guided the way for planes flying at night. At that time, night flights were unusual. When we were lost and needed directions, one of the hunting party would climb a tall tree and look for the rotating airport light. If we found the light, we knew it was east from our hunting area. Once we found east, we then knew north, and our way home was simple.

*Vanished! Half the world's wildlife population.*
– WORLD WILDLIFE ORGANIZATION

# A PUT-DOWN TO LAST
# A LIFETIME

DURING MY YEARS AT KILLEEN HIGH SCHOOL (1936–1939), I found that I was a poor algebra student, but geometry came more easily for me. I understood its purpose and could explain the procedure in solving the geometry problems.

Killeen was a very small school when I attended high school. In total, there were about 325 students enrolled in the entire school system. My graduating class was around thirty-five students. At that time, the superintendent of the school normally taught one class. Yes, he was my math teacher.

The star athlete, Jack Arnold, had the same problem in geometry as I did in algebra. We were friends, and from time to time, I could offer an explanation that would increase his understanding of a geometry problem.

I remember one time when Jack was called upon to place a problem on the board and explain the process in solving it. Jack gave a commendable explanation of the solution process. The teacher/superintendent exclaimed, "Jack, that is a fine explanation! It seems you are beginning to understand the geometry concept."

Jack replied, "Thanks, but I had help in solving the problem."

The superintendent replied, "Well, who gave you the help?"

"Norman Hall."

The superintendent said, "Norman Hall? I am surprised that he would be able to help anyone—and certainly not with a geometry problem."

At that point, the entire class laughed and turned to look at me. His response did not anger me – I suppose because, at least, my ability in geometry had been recognized. But I never forgot the statement made by the teacher/superintendent that day. As the years went by, I did come to resent the context of the statement, especially after I became a teacher.

While serving in the army, I was training to be in the glider's troops. We were instructed that the most frightening phase of glider troop activities occurred when the glider was cut loose from the DC-3 plane. That was the time to begin searching for a place to land. The glider ratio was 15:1; this meant that for every fifteen feet you moved forward, the glider would drop one foot, a geometric concept I clearly understood. Common gossip among the experienced glider troops was that during that time of descent, you would do one of three things: pray, think of your mother, or think of someone you hated.

Without pause, I immediately thought of my geometry teacher.

After leaving the service, I returned to Killeen, and I served as a principal for sixteen years. During this time, I earned a master's degree and later a doctoral degree.

At that same time, my geometry teacher/ superintendent stepped down from that position and became our business manager. Not once did he ever call me Doctor.

I suppose the put-down was not so bad after all. During thirty-seven years of filling speaking engagements all over the nation, I earned $329,627 as a speaker.

Hit me again, teacher!

*Life is a book unwritten; only you hold the pen.*
– UNKNOWN

# LEARNING TO DANCE

AFTER A LONG PERIOD OF LIVING ON THE RANCH WITHOUT indoor bathroom facilities, we moved to town. This created a new experience for me: I learned to dance while waiting for my two brothers to finish using the bathroom.

*Attitude is more important than the past, than education,*
*than money, than circumstances, than what people do or say.*
*It is more important than appearance, giftedness, or skill.*
– R. SWINDOLL

# STILL WEAR MY COAT

As you can imagine, when living on a ranch during the 1920s and 1930s, one experienced very few luxuries. For example, the toilet was some distance from the house. This presented a problem when it was raining, storming, or cold. It seemed to have made a lasting impression on me. At age ninety-four, I still wear my coat when I go to the bathroom.

*People are a product of their environment.*
– UNKNOWN

# FIGHTING ON THE SCHOOL BUS
## (according to Billye)

ONE OF THE REAL ACCOMPLISHMENTS IN MY LIFE WAS that I married Billye Barr. However, there were times when such an accomplishment did seem doubtful.

There was a year when we rode the same school bus. Billye's account includes the recollection that for a considerable period of time, she did not know what I looked like. According to her, I was always in the back of the bus, fighting—and I was always on the bottom.

*Be*
*someone's reason*
*to*
*smile.*
– UNKNOWN

# I'LL WAIT FOR YOU

DURING MY YEARS IN SCHOOL, I RODE A SCHOOL BUS TO and from school each day. When I was a junior in high school, I noticed a pretty girl who had also started riding the bus. She must have been in middle school. One thing I noticed especially was the armload of books she carried home day after day.

Her name was Billye Barr.

As days passed, I became more and more fascinated with how pretty she was. On one occasion, I sat next to her and engaged in conversation. I told her I thought she was very pretty and that I would wait for her to grow up if she wanted to get married. She only smiled and turned away to speak to someone else.

For the balance of my junior year in high school and on through my senior year, we would exchange tongue-in-cheek expressions about me waiting for her. At the beginning when I told her I would wait for her to grow up, she would only smile. As time went by, she responded with "We will see" or "Are you really waiting?"

I graduated from high school and went on to college. I did not see her for an extended period of time. When I graduated from college, I returned home and saw Billye Barr for the first time in three years. She was no longer pretty—she was beautiful! She was the first to say, "Are you still waiting?"

I said, "I sure am!"

We started dating, and we were married a year later. That was the beginning of more than seventy-three years of wedded bliss.

We had two fine sons and enjoyed life on a ranch for a time. The boys remember this as a high point of their childhoods. Billye and I enjoyed traveling to different countries. We felt we had traveled the world. We enjoyed our life together to the fullest.

*The best way to predict your future is to create it.*
– ABRAHAM LINCOLN

# PROPHET OR LUCKY?

I RODE A BUS TO SCHOOL EVERY DAY BECAUSE WE LIVED out in the country. The route in the afternoon was long, so to break the monotony, some of the boys would get off at the crossroads and wait until the bus made the return trip down the same road.

There was also a very pretty, popular girl on the bus. She was a freshman who was in band, and she was also a cheerleader and an athlete who played tennis and softball. One afternoon, I announced to the group of boys that I was going to marry that girl, Billye Barr. The group laughed and laughed at the idea that I thought I could ever marry Billye Barr.

As time moved on, I went away to college for four years. In the meantime, Camp Hood was established near Killeen. Almost everything changed in my life except my desire to marry Billye Barr. My dream finally came true. We married two days before I left for military duty.

Almost twenty years later in California, we had dinner

with an old schoolmate. During the dinner, he looked at me and said, "Well, you did it!"

I replied, "Did what?"

"Married Billye," he said, "the queen of Killeen."

He told Billye about the statement I had made long ago on the bus route. This was the first she had heard about my secret plans for her. My plan worked out really well. On July 6, 2013, we celebrated our seventieth wedding anniversary.

*Do not follow where the path may lead. Go instead where there is no path and leave a trail.*
– RALPH WALDO EMERSON

# RATTLESNAKE INN

IN KILLEEN, TEXAS, DURING THE 1930S, WE CALLED THE movie theater the "picture show." They had movies on Friday, Saturday, and Sunday nights. The only afternoon movie was on Saturday.

Killeen was a dry town, which meant there was no alcohol sold in the town. However, sixteen miles away, one could visit the only honky-tonk around: the Rattlesnake Inn. That place had a reputation of being a pretty rough night spot back then. Rumor had it that as you entered the club, they would search you for a weapon—and if you did not have one, they would give you one.

*In the truest sense, freedom cannot be bestowed; it must be achieved.*
– FRANKLIN D. ROOSEVELT

# FIVE WAS NOT ENOUGH

BACK IN THE 1920S, THERE WERE NO STATEWIDE RULES or regulations as to when a student could start the first grade. These decisions were left up to the individual school districts.

I had a cousin who was six years old, and she planned to start school in September of 1927. I was only five years old and wanted to start school when she did. My mother was concerned about this, so she went to see Miss Anna Mary Gilmore, the first-grade teacher for the last twenty years. Together they decided I could start school at age five.

It was a mistake! I never caught up. All through the eleven grades of school, Jean Bowen, my cousin, led the class in most of the scholastic endeavors. When the order of achievement was reversed, I led the class.

Even in college, I felt I never overcame the lack of background I missed in my grade-school years. My educational growth finally occurred during the four years, nineteen days, and about thirty minutes I spent in the army. This was one reason I felt compelled to pursue an education. Once I was discharged from the service, I continued my education and received a master's degree in 1949 and a doctor of education degree in 1960.

I have never been able to pinpoint exactly what I missed by starting to school at age five, but the feeling that I was always behind other students academically haunted me for over twenty years. The doctor's degree gave me a welcome sigh of relief.

*Most people, teachers and administrators included,*
*do not fully understand how learning happens.*
– GALE BARTOW

# College Stories

I began college at Texas A&M in 1939. After two years when I ran out of money, I taught school for a year before returning to college. I graduated from A&M in 1943. After graduation, I entered the army for four years during World War II.

*I must study politics and war, that our sons may have liberty to study mathematics and philosophy.*
– JOHN ADAMS

# FREIGHT TRAINS IN MY LIFE

AFTER MY FRESHMAN YEAR OF COLLEGE AT TEXAS A&M, J. L. Williams, my roommate, and I decided we would attend summer school at Tarleton College in Stephenville, Texas, about seventy miles from Fort Worth. We took courses in English and genetics.

The genetics class had a lab once a week at the college farm located about five miles from the campus. Since neither of us had a car, the best way for us to get there was to walk down the railroad tracks that went by the college farm. One time as we started to walk to the farm, we heard a freight train approaching and decided we should hop the freight and ride it to the farm. We were amazed at the speed the train picked up in the five short miles. By the time the train arrived at the farm, it seemed to be going more than fifty miles per hour – too fast for us to jump off. The train did not slow down at any point until it reached Fort Worth. There we took a taxi to the highway heading west toward Stephenville and were able to catch rides to our destination. We arrived around seven o'clock that evening having completely missed our lab class.

The next summer, J.L. and I decided we would like to go to Mexico. Neither of us had ever been out of the state, so we thought going to Mexico would be a great experience. We hitchhiked from College Station to El Paso with little trouble. We then spent two days in El Paso before we crossed the border into Juarez.

We started our trip back home by standing on the highway thumbing a ride. Shortly, a car stopped. The driver said he was going to Alpine and would be glad to give us a ride. Neither of us had ever heard of Alpine, so we said okay. What we did not know was that Alpine was almost a hundred miles south of our direct route home.

We arrived in Alpine in late morning and immediately started thumbing a ride toward Fort Stockton. A number of drivers stopped and offered rides, but their destinations were only a few miles out of town. We spent from late morning to almost seven o'clock thumbing with no success. During the day, we had made the acquaintance of the operator of a service station near where we had placed ourselves on the highway. Around seven o'clock, we heard a train approaching Alpine. The man at the station asked us if we would consider riding a freight train. He said the train would go to Fort Stockton and on to San Antonio, and he volunteered to take us to the freight yard. When we arrived, the train was moving slowly to a stop. We boarded a boxcar and were ready for a leisurely trip back to civilization.

The empty boxcar we had picked had been hauling wheat. The procedure for transporting wheat was to line the boxcar with brown paper along the walls and even the floor to prevent wheat from sifting out through any cracks. As the train moved along and through the Davis Mountains, it became cold. J. L. tore some of the paper from the walls, placed the paper in the corner of the car, and lit a fire. What he was not prepared for was that the paper on the walls and floor also caught fire. For a short period of time, we were in an inferno, but the smoke provided the greatest hazard. We lay on the floor with our faces hanging out the door so we could breathe free of smoke. As we lay there, the wind caused burning paper to land on our backs and legs, so we had to take turns patting the burning paper off each other. This drama only lasted a few minutes, but it was an experience we would never forget. By the way, it did not seem cold during the rest of the ride.

We spent the night in Fort Stockton and returned to the highway the next morning.

After these two train riding experiences, I considered myself an experienced hobo.

When I was in college, Killeen was a small ranching and farming community located thirty miles between Temple and Lampasas. Both of those communities had main roads leading north and south, but Killeen had no roads going those directions. For a college boy needing to thumb his way, this presented a problem. Because a traveling salesman would most likely stay in Temple or Lampasas for a night on the road, little if any traffic passed between Temple and Lampasas after 5:00 p.m. Any hitchhiker going to Killeen needed to be thumbing it before five in the afternoon. Many times, as I hitchhiked home, I would arrive in Temple after that time. My salvation was the 11:20 p.m. freight train that went from Temple through Killeen to Lampasas. Once again, I became a hobo.

The problem was the train usually picked up speed as it rode the tracks downhill just out of Killeen. I caught this train a number of times during my junior and senior years of college, so I was prepared to jump from the fast-moving train. I had a small, old cardboard suitcase that I carried for a cushion when I jumped. I placed it under my chin, with the main part covering my chest. I usually hit the ground on my feet, but sometimes the momentum going forward caused me to hit the ground with the suitcase first. The suitcase protected my chin and suffered the most damage. I usually had to pick up socks, shorts, or even a shirt from the ground where I landed. At times, I even had to go back during daylight the next day to retrieve a lost article or two.

Would you believe me if I told you I have not ridden a freight train since my senior year of college?

*Education is not preparation for life; education is life itself.*
– JOHN DEWEY

# SELLING THE MILK COWS

ONCE I STARTED COLLEGE, I TRIED TO ADAPT TO COLLEGE life, and I participated in athletics and social events. I suppose the social aspect of my new way of life took precedence over everything else. This took more money than I was accustomed to spending, and I should have been concerned when the family money available for my tuition and fees was spent to purchase secondhand elements of the specific ROTC uniform and textbooks.

The solution to my need for increased funds to pay for my social activities was to write to my mother and state the amount of cash needed for any upcoming activity. There was little hesitation on her part in responding to my requests. Only occasionally did she ask for more information as to why the expenditure was necessary or beneficial to my activities.

It was well into the second semester of my freshman year—perhaps late February or early March—when I returned home for a weekend visit. I had, as usual, used my thumb ("highwayed") to make the trip.

Late that Friday afternoon as I was walking down the main street of Killeen, I met a third cousin who was much older than I. He was a bookkeeper at the only combination grocery and dry-goods store in town, the same store where my mother was employed for years. As was customary in a small town in those days, he knew our family history and, I suppose, a great deal of the financial condition of the Hall family.

He asked about college and inquired as to why I was home. After passing the time of day with a few other comments, he asked me to follow him somewhere. "I would like to show you something," he said.

The business section of Killeen was only five city blocks long and four blocks wide. In the early days, all the stores on Main Street faced the railroad. The stock pens remained active as a part of the economy of the community. As cars became a way of life, the stores reversed their front doors and faced the city's main street.

He led me to the stockyard, where there was only

one animal, a milk cow. He asked, "Do you recognize that cow?"

I replied, "No, I don't suppose I do."

To that statement, he said, "You should. It was one of your folks' milk cows. When you started to college, they had five very productive milk cows. This is the fourth one they have sold to send you money for college. They only have one left." He did not place judgment on my activities and made no comment other than, "I thought you ought to know." With that, he walked off back to town.

This was not only a shock for me, but it caused a heavy feeling of guilt to come over me. Our family had always been close. I was younger by ten years than my two brothers. I had been home and witnessed the struggle many farm families had and were still going through. I stayed at the stock pens for a considerable amount of time. I revisited in my own mind what I gained by my excessive expenditures. I realized how little I gained in attending the meaningless social activities.

I considered dropping out of college and going to work, but I knew my mother would not allow it. She was intent on my receiving a college education. I knew dropping out would hurt her and cause her to feel that I had not done my part in fulfilling her plans for me.

I returned to college with a new attitude and got a job as a janitor. I was assigned to provide custodial service to the third floor of the chemistry building. With this job, I was able to earn enough money to pay for my meals. After two years as a janitor, I became a waiter in the dining hall. This job paid my room and board. I worked there until I graduated.

Neither my mother nor my father ever mentioned the sale of the milk cows, and I never mentioned my visit to the stockyards. However, during my senior year, a few weeks before graduation, they told me that they appreciated me bearing some of the load involved in my college education. That statement meant more to me than the diploma.

*We want to write the word "success" too soon.*
*It should be kept for the epitaph.*
– HENRY FORD

# COUNTRY BOY TO THE LIBRARY

I ATTENDED ALL MY ELEVEN YEARS OF PUBLIC SCHOOL IN Killeen, Texas. The total enrollment of the school was 324. Of them, 132 students were enrolled in high school grades eight to eleven. The school was in a three-story red-brick building. The primary grades were on the first floor, the grammar school grades four to seven were on the second floor, and the high school was on the third floor.

I thought the study hall was a huge room because it was larger than any of the other rooms in the building. The library was in the corner, near the front of the room. Latticework separated it from the study hall. There was a small open window in the latticework that was used to check out books. Miss Genie was the librarian, and it was said that she had every book neatly filed on the shelves of the library except one—and she was looking for that one. Book cards were placed in a wooden Velveeta cheese box. The books had no numbers, and you requested a book by title. Miss Genie knew exactly where it was and would get it for you. This was all very efficient.

I felt I had mastered the book checkout process at Killeen High School. However, that was not the case when I entered Texas A&M College in 1939. A month or so into the semester, one professor made an assignment that would require research at the library. Like a good freshman cadet, I inquired as to the location of the library. I was sure I was given incorrect information when the person I asked pointed to a large, three-story brick building in the middle of the campus. Since that was the only information I had about the library, I approached the building. Upon entering, I did not see a single bookshelf or even a book. There were about a dozen cabinets located in a large open area, each having about a dozen small drawers. There was a long counter with at least four people working behind it. As I approached the counter, one of the people asked if he could help me. I replied by giving him the title of the two books I needed. His reply was that he needed the book number. I said, "Where do I get the book number?"

With a frown or maybe even with an expression of disgust, he said, "From the card catalog, of course."

I looked around and did not see a single Velveeta box or a Sears and Roebuck catalog. So I left without any information. It was hard, but I finished my sophomore year without ever going back to the library.

By the time I entered my junior year, I had been exposed to many more professors and academically successful students than I had during my early years at A&M. I began to understand the open- and closed-stack library system. By then, I learned that Miss Genie had operated a closed-stack system without card catalogs.

*Learning changes everything.*
– MCGRAW EDUCATION NEWSLETTER

# SHORT-TERM FRIENDS

WHEN I FINISHED HIGH SCHOOL, MY MOTHER INSISTED that I go to college. She made sure my two older brothers attended college, even though times were hard and money was scarce. When I embarked upon my early college career, I was reading on probably a fifth-grade level and did not know the multiplication tables.

Few students had cars in those days, and often the sides of highways had many people with their thumbs out asking for a ride. Luckily for me, my parents decided to drive the 140 miles to Texas A&M in College Station, Texas, to help get me set up in my assigned room in Dormitory Unit Two in the Duncan Mess Hall area on campus.

We all went to the dorm to locate my room before unloading my belongings. As we entered the first floor, we passed a room with an opened door. We saw four boys inside who were in uniforms and seemed to be upperclassmen. When we passed, two of the boys came out of the room and asked if they could help. My mother responded that I was a new student and we were looking for my assigned room. They readily showed us room 215 on the second floor.

They even offered to bring in my footlocker, other boxes, and my hang-up clothes. By then, all four of the boys were helping and engaging in conversation with both my mother and dad. They offered information as to the location of the dining hall, the post office, and the drill field. They also offered some of the names of the buildings where my classes would likely be scheduled. After placing my belongings in the room, the four boys returned to their room and allowed me several minutes to say good-bye to my parents. After a short time, my folks drove away from the dorm and headed toward home. My mother had been very impressed with the politeness and friendliness of the boys we had met. She thought I was fortunate to be in a dorm with such nice young men.

After my parents drove away, I returned to the room of the four young men to get better acquainted. Upon entering the room, I expressed my appreciation for their help and for the politeness they had shown my parents. At that moment, I learned much about the life of a freshman on the campus at Texas A&M. I was informed in no uncertain terms what was expected of a dumb freshman. I was to address all upperclassmen as *sir* and stand at attention when any conversation took place between me and any upperclassman.

What had happened to those friendly and polite guys? I thought of running to catch my folks and returning home, but by then I was standing at attention. In such a short time, I was advised that my company would stand formation and march to all meals and sit in assigned seats. I would always wear a white strip of cloth on the cuff of my shirt to let all know I was a dumb freshman. Not only would I clean my own room each day but also the room of an assigned senior. My extra uniform hanging in the closet of my room would have all buttons buttoned. I would place my class schedule on my door so the sophomores would know my whereabouts at all times.

This was my introduction to being in the corps of cadets at Texas A&M. With time and close association with my classmates, a strong bond was formed. As I was told, I was to trade one miserable freshman year for three great years as an upperclassman. I graduated in May of '43 and had already been inducted into the army in June of 1942. Even after all these years, I am still drawn to the campus with a strong interest in the accomplishments of the university, the corps, and the athletic programs. It is such a great institution. I owe so much to the university. Any success I had during my professional career had its beginnings in those years at Texas A&M. I graduated with a bachelor's and master's degree from Texas A&M. A few years later, I received a doctoral degree from the University of Northern Colorado (formerly Colorado State College).

*Bill Gates, the world's richest college dropout, says stay in school.*
– SAN ANTONIO KSAT

# THE SPEECH TEACHER

As a sophomore in college, I decided I needed to improve my grade-point average, so I began searching the college catalogue for classes that might lend themselves to an easy grade. I found one: Speech 101. I thought, *This is a natural for me.* I could talk, and that seemed to me to be all Speech 101 might be—just talk.

I quickly signed up for the course. The first several weeks were devoted to speech preparation, selecting a topic, organization of the materials, and speech delivery. As I had expected, there were no tests, no pressure, and no homework. It was really a coasting course. Soon the day came when speech topics were assigned and a schedule of presentations was posted.

When my presentation time came, I had applied all the presented steps in preparing my topic. I took my position at the front of the class and delivered what I thought was an acceptable speech.

After more than fifty years, I vividly remember the way

that teacher was dressed. She had a bright piece of cloth as part of her hairstyle. She had light-blue beads around her neck. Her dress was almost white with orange-colored diamond designs woven into the material. She wore light-blue shoes. (This fascinated me because my mother only wore black shoes.)

I returned to my desk and waited for the critique of my presentation.

"Thank you, Mr. Hall," she said. "I appreciate your effort. You will never be a public speaker, but I appreciate you trying."

The statement certainly captured my attention because it was made before the entire class. It did not devastate me, but I never forgot her words. That might be part of the reason I devoted part of my adult life to motivational speaking. For more than thirty years, it was a part of my livelihood. I started making free presentations and later charged fifty dollars. I also remember when I increased my fee to seventy-five dollars. In time, I was speaking on what was called a "speaking circuit," where the fees increased from $100 up to $2,500 in my later years of speaking. Over a thirty-year period, I earned $329,627 as a motivational speaker in the U.S., Mexico, and Canada.

Every time I sit on the stage, waiting to be introduced, I always think about what the speech teacher said so many years ago. I am sure a twinkle appears in my eyes as I take the podium.

I daresay many teachers have no idea of the impact a few words of praise or criticism can have on a student.

*Practice doesn't make perfect, but it does increase the chance for success.*
– UNKNOWN

# A MULE IN THE
# FOURTH-FLOOR SHOWER

IN MY TIME AT TEXAS A&M, A FRESHMAN WAS OFTEN told he was the lowest form of humanity. We were made to feel we had no purpose, no dignity, and no future. The school was all military, and campus description was built around this concept.

As freshmen, many of us thought sophomores were created with the main purpose of thinking up outlandish things for us to do. For example, the sophomores in our dorm decided it would be worthwhile for a group of freshmen to get a mule from a nearby farm and take it to the fourth-floor restroom of our dorm and place it in the shower.

We started with about an eight-member team. However, before the task was done, we needed four more strong bodies. It was a struggle because one of us had to keep biting the mule's ear. (We were told by a sophomore that this would calm him to some extent.) Three of us were pulling on the rope around the mule's neck while the other eight members were on the mule's side or pushing him from the rear. Each of us had been kicked at least four times, and our feet were stepped on a dozen or more times. We were also bounced into the walls more times than we cared to count.

Of course, when the seniors discovered the mule in the shower, bedlam took over dorm number two. This triggered a chain reaction. The seniors fought the juniors. The juniors fought with the sophomores, and the sophomores really got after the freshmen.

I thought it was hard getting the mule up the three flights of stairs, but trying to convince a mule to go *down* three flights of stairs was even harder.

Being a freshman at Texas A&M was a memorable experience, especially after the year was over. My experiences at A&M during my freshman, sophomore, junior, and senior years resulted in a lifetime of pride for me, toward other students, and in the institution. Looking back, I know I would not be the same person I am today if I had not attended A&M.

*Never underestimate the power of stupid people in large groups.*
– GEORGE CARLIN

# WHAT MIGHT HAVE BEEN: THE STORY OF THE BROWN JUG

IF YOU WALKED INTO MY OFFICE AT ANY TIME DURING the past forty years and even today, you would see an old brown jug in a prominent location on the credenza behind my desk. Its constant presence has had a profound impact on my life. It rekindles a memory of days long past.

As a boy raised on a ranch, some of my summer jobs involved field work, such as chopping cotton, gathering corn, heading maize, and picking cotton. In those days, I am sure I lacked ambition, and I had an attitude to prove it.

Summers in central Texas have always been hot and dry, and often, an uncomfortably warm, swirling wind blew dust around you. All of this brought misery to the long days we worked at the ranch. I remember going each day to the field with a tow sack-covered brown jug filled with water. Water was also used to saturate the tow sack that covered the jug to keep the water in the jug as cool as possible. I usually placed the jug ten rows from where I started work. My whole objective for the next hour was to get to the jug for a drink of water. When I accomplished that, I would place the jug ten more rows away. My entire day was designed to reach the water jug. This summer activity went on year after year while I was in junior high and a large part of my high school years.

I did not particularly want to go to college, but my mother insisted. While I was there, I suppose a spark of ambition was stirred. Then, after four years in the army, I found I had a very strong desire to have meaning and purpose in my life.

A few years later, I found an old brown jug much like the one I had used on the ranch. I have kept it in view at my offices because it symbolizes my life on the ranch where I was working ten rows at a time. As a young person, I did not realize I had begun to develop my character. I was setting goals and reaching them, one row at a time.

Today, I am a multimillionaire with a PhD, a wonderful wife, and two fine sons. My family means the world to me. The jug serves as a reminder of the days gone by.

*Education is not the means of showing people how to get what they want. Education is an exercise by means of which enough men, it is hoped, will learn to want what is worth having.*
– RONALD REAGAN

# THE DE SOTO ROCK

A FEW MILES FROM KILLEEN, THERE WAS ONCE A LARGE stand-alone hill that we called Castle Mountain. It was the size of two football fields and was high enough to prevent any four-wheeled vehicles from going to the top.

The Castle was covered with trees, brush, rock ledges, and prickly pear cactus. Years ago, someone discovered a large rock on Castle Mountain, and they called it the de Soto Rock. It was the size of two large stuffed pillows, and it had the words "De Soto" carved into it. Below the words was a date: 1556.

According to legend and history, De Soto was a Spanish explorer who explored Texas in the 1500s. He led the first explorers into the southern parts of today's United States. His expeditions crossed the Mississippi River in search of gold and silver. He was also searching for a passage to China. Some research indicates that his expeditions came as far as what are now the Waco and Austin areas. He died of a fever on the west side of the Mississippi

River near what is now Ferriday, Louisiana, on May 21, 1542. After his death, his expedition split into several groups. One group wanted to return overland to Florida. Another group wanted to remain near the mouth of the Mississippi River in hopes of contacting another ship. The third group started overland to Mexico City. It is this last group that some historians believe might have made the carving on the Castle Mountain rock. History records indicate that this group, without leadership or supplies, spent years living with the Indians before resuming their journey to Mexico City.

The rock had long been forgotten—until the 1920s, when Billye Barr's family moved to the farm where the de Soto Rock was located. As a teenager, she discovered the rock again. A new excitement arose in our community, and countless individuals came to see the rediscovered rock.

In 1941, the word came to the community of Killeen that the army was planning to build an army camp in our area. Much of the land would be taken as a training area. As a former history teacher, I thought about the de Soto Rock. I built a small sled out of two-inch-by-four-inch lumber. With a great amount of help, we loaded the rock on the sled and pulled it to my car. I took it to my dad's ranch and hid it in an area where I thought it would be safe. Later, I learned that the area where the rock had once been was taken into the Camp Hood expansion.

Several years later, I went back to see if I could find the rock. I found it on Dad's old place, and so had someone else. Below de Soto's name was a new carving: "Kilroy was here."

The de Soto Rock is now in the museum at Fort Hood.

*Every great mistake has a halfway moment—a split second when it can be recalled and perhaps remedied.*
– PAUL S. BUCK

# AN EIGHTEEN-WHEELER

WHILE I WAS ATTENDING TEXAS A&M IN THE 1930S AND 1940s, a common mode of travel was to thumb a ride with a passing motorist. We referred to it as "highwaying it." This was a very effective method for student travel.

One Saturday morning in April, my roommate and I decided to highway it to our hometown in Killeen. Things went as usual. We caught a ride from Bryan to Caldwell, another ride from Caldwell to Cameron, and another ride to Belton. By this time, it was dark, and rides became scarce. Time passed with no luck until ten o'clock, when a large eighteen-wheeler flatbed truck stopped.

The driver of the truck got out to talk to us. I was very impressed by his appearance. He was at least six feet, eight inches tall and probably weighed 250 pounds. He was a very impressive figure of a man.

He explained that we were welcome to ride, but we would need to ride on the flatbed of the truck because there was no room in the cab. He told us that two large spare truck tires were bolted to the truck bed, and we should be safe if we sat inside the tires.

After having already waited over four hours for a ride, we thought his offer seemed inviting, so we climbed onto the truck. Thus, the wild and windy ride began. Riding on a flatbed truck at speeds up to sixty miles an hour was a scary—but memorable—experience. We passed cars and other eighteen-wheelers. My roommate lost his cap, and I lost my briefcase.

As we arrived in Killeen, the driver pulled to the side of the road and stopped. When he was walking toward us he said, "Well, are you two still there?" To this day, his words reverberate in my head. Why did he think we wouldn't still be there?

I actually recognized the driver. I had known of him for several years. My older brother had taught him in one of the country schools near Killeen. I could not remember his real name, so as we disembarked from the truck bed I said, "Thanks a lot, Shorty."

My roommate said, "Let's get out of here fast. He doesn't like being called Shorty!"

Sometime later, I saw the driver in a café. As I approached him, I asked if I could call him Shorty.

His reply was short and very meaningful. "No!"

I replied, "Thank you, Mr. Cosper."

*I have learned more from people who didn't agree with me than all the people who did agree with me*
– NORMAN HALL

# CAREER CHOICES

IF I TOLD YOU I WAS AN AVERAGE STUDENT WHILE attending public school, I would be stretching the truth to its limits. My mother insisted that her three sons would each attend college, even in the years of economic depression. As I prepared to go to college, I examined the college catalog with the reference to course requirements.

I discovered a major in sociology required no chemistry and very little math. At the time, this seemed like a worthy cause. Upon entering college, I chose sociology as my major.

During my sophomore year, I visited with one of the sociology professors. "Dr. Russel," I asked, "what kind of work does a sociology major do when they finish college?"

Dr. Russel paused for a minute before answering. "They usually go home and help their fathers."

Since I did not think my father needed any help on the ranch, I changed my major to agriculture administration. The prospect for employment then seemed much brighter.

*It's never too late to be who you might have been.*
– GEORGE ELLIOTT

# THE SPIRIT BY MY SIDE

I GREW UP AS WHAT YOU MIGHT CALL A COUNTRY BOY. I lived on a ranch in an isolated area of Bell County, Texas. Our nearest neighbor was two miles away. The road leading to the ranch was not even graveled. The telephone was on a party line of eight customers. We had no radio or television or water piped into the kitchen. Our main source of contact with the rest of the world was the rural mail carrier. The public schools in Killeen provided no bus transportation at the time. I played with eight or so Mexican children who also lived on the ranch. As a result, I learned to speak Spanish.

My mother had a goal of seeing her three sons finish college with a degree of their choosing. I was the youngest son, but I lacked the desire and ability to be a college student. It was a challenge for my mother and me. "We" made it through high school and earned a bachelor's degree from Texas A&M.

After four years in the army during World War II,

I returned to civilian life with a fresh attitude toward education. I realized that education could change everything. I continued my education immediately after military service. I received a master's degree. Then, about six years later, I became interested in earning a doctoral degree.

My mother had supported me at every turn of my educational endeavors with strong encouragement and, from time to time, financial support. It took me six years to earn the doctorate because I had to go during the summer and two spring terms.

When I walked across the stage to receive my doctoral degree, I was not walking alone. I felt the spirit of my mother was by my side. She had done so much to get me to this point – she deserved to be there.

*Do all the good you can. By all the means you can. In all the ways you can. In all the places you can. At all the times you can. To all the people you can. As long as ever you can.*
– JOHN WESLEY, EIGHTEENTH-CENTURY THEOLOGIAN

# MISSPELLING AT A HIGH LEVEL

DURING THE 1960S, I WAS ATTENDING COLLEGE TO WORK on my doctoral degree. I had completed all the required coursework and was devoting my time to writing the required dissertation which had a value of eighteen college course hours.

It was a large and tedious process that forgave few if any mistakes. At the end of one summer, I completed the draft of the dissertation and submitted it to my major professor for his approval. After his approval, the last step was to present the dissertation to the all-powerful graduate committee. Upon their approval, I would be awarded a doctoral degree in educational administration.

On the appointed day and time, I returned to the major professor's office after his evaluation of my work. His greeting to me was, "Norm, you misspelled seventeen words in your dissertation draft, and incidentally, it was the same word all seventeen times."

I had misspelled the word *misspelled* using one "s" rather than two. My only defense was that I only misspelled one word.

The professor's reply was, "Yes, but you did it seventeen times!"

I rewrote the parts of the dissertation in question.

*If you have a problem to solve in an hour, spend fifty-five minutes defining the problem.*
– UNKNOWN

# My Family's Stories

These family stories span from the mid-1940s until the early 1960s when my family bought our own ranch seven miles south of Killeen. The setting of some of the stories included is the community of Lake McQueeney, where I now live.

*Never doubt that a small group of thoughtful, concerned citizens can change the world. Indeed, it is the only thing that ever has.*
– MARGARET MEAD

# THE RANCH BRAND

THE HALL RANCH NEAR SUGARLOAF MOUNTAIN IN central Texas has been in existence since the 1850s. Although it has changed size and boundaries a number of times, it continued to be a landmark in the area.

Over the years, the ranch brand has changed from a single H to an H with rockers on each leg. This produced a brand like ℍ.

This symbol of ownership captured the imagination of Caleb, one of our grandsons. He had the brand tattooed on the upper portion of his right arm. Another grandson followed suit, along with his father. Thus, the brand lives on, even today.

Dock and Lola Hall, the last owners of the ranch before Fort Hood expanded to the shores of Belton Lake, would be very proud of the efforts of these three to preserve the memory of the brand.

*My forefathers didn't come over on the*
*Mayflower, but they met the boat.*
– WILL ROGERS

# KINFOLK

I SUPPOSE EVERYONE HAS A VARIETY OF KINFOLK. I know I sure do. I have records that go back to the 1870s.

Not long after the end of the Civil War, a long, winding road was built some nine miles northeast of Killeen, a town that had sprung up on the new rail line heading west from Temple. Along this road, seven Hall families owned land and established log-cabin residences. Each family had possessions including range cows, milk cows, horses, pigs, and goats. The homes along the road were referred to as Hall Town.

As time passed, one of the families decided to move west to look for greener pastures. They sold some of their furniture and livestock. Then they packed their wagon, gathered their livestock, and said their good-byes. They departed on a Sunday night.

By late Wednesday, the remaining Hall ranches began to notice missing livestock. In all, they counted six range cows, two milk cows, a horse, and two calves as missing, but by then, they realized what had happened to the livestock.

A family posse was formed and set out to overtake their kinfolk. It took several days, but they made contact west of what is now San Saba County. There is no record of what happened to their relatives; however, the livestock was returned to its rightful owners.

This incident fits into my family history as the reason behind the formation of a cattle-branding iron. My great-grandfather's family was one of the seven families living in Hall Town when the livestock was stolen. He always used an H iron to brand his cattle. However, when the posse overtook the stolen property, he discovered how easily the brand could be changed. His H had been changed into an H4 brand that is now referred to as an H4 brand. The man who stole the animals had used the H brand and added the 4 to it. By placing the 4 along the side of the brand that was already on the animal, he created the H4 brand.

When Granddad returned home, he took the H brands and placed a "tail" on each leg of the H brand.

Thereby, the Ħ brand was born. Even today, some 130 years later, the family still uses the brand for the three ranches owned by the descendants of Hall Town.

*It's not what you look at that matters. It's what you see.*

# MY MOTHER'S HANDS

I WANT TO TELL YOU ABOUT MY MOTHER'S HANDS. OH, I know. They were scarred, old, and wrinkled, and my story is how they got that way.

When I was perhaps five or six years old, I had climbed a large tree. When I decided to get down, I was holding on to a large limb. I looked down and discovered that I was directly above a barbed-wire fence. I called for a playmate to go get my mother. When she arrived, without hesitation, she held her arms out over the fence and said, "Turn loose, son. I'll catch you." I let go. My weight drove her arms and hands into the barbs on the fence, which resulted in two large cuts on both hands.

When living on a ranch, there always seem to be encounters involving horses, cows, or goats. One day, just after I started attending school, I crossed through the goat corral. A billy goat with wide, sharp horns ran over and butted me down. Mother suddenly appeared. She wrestled the goat to the ground and held him until I could run to the rail fence. Mother released the goat. When she came to see about me, her hands and arms were bleeding.

Another time, Mother and I were in the garden, harvesting potatoes. (To harvest potatoes, one must dig in the ground.) As I went from plant to plant on my knees, I came face to face with a coiled snake. I was so frightened that I froze. I could not move myself away from the snake. By this time, the snake was ready to strike. Mother reached around me and pulled me away. The snake struck her right hand, and she pulled back. I feared the worst, but as it turned out, the snake was not venomous. I am always reminded that she did not know that when she placed herself in harm's way.

Several years later, I had grown to the extent that I could help with the ranch chores. We were branding cattle, and my job was to rope the cows and pull them up to the fire where the branding irons were heated. This went well for hours. On one occasion, I had to pull the calf to the fire where the people doing the branding took the animal and threw it on its side. I had started to dismount from my horse when one of the cowboys dropped the red-hot branding iron on the arm of the man holding down the calf. He let out a scream and jumped to his feet. This frightened my horse, who jumped back and jerked away. This caused me to fall from the horse. My foot hung in the stirrup, and I was helpless as the horse ran away in fear. My mother, who had been serving coffee to the ranch hands, was standing near the fire. She dropped the coffeepot, grabbed the reins of the horse, and reached up to take hold of the bit to control the animal. In so doing, the horse bit her hand. This forced the bit deeper into the horse's mouth. With the help of the ranch hands, she was able to bring the horse under control, and I was then able to free my foot from the stirrup. The wounds Mother suffered from this event lasted for months because an infection delayed the healing process.

These and many other similar events involving my two brothers and me accounted for the condition of her hands. Mother dedicated her adult life to selflessly raising and protecting her three sons.

*The mother's heart is the child's schoolroom.*
– HENRY WARD BEECHER

# THE MEANING OF HALT

WHEN THE BOUNDARIES OF FORT HOOD WERE established in west Bell County, Texas, in 1941, a part of the east boundary bordered our ranch. Therefore, in order to get home from Killeen, we had to take a road that ran through a part of the Fort Hood Reservation.

In time, along the reservation road, the army built a modest airfield that was home to small observation planes. As the war ended, increased activity at the airfield inspired the expansion of the airfield facilities.

Billye and I lived in Killeen, and my mother worked in town. From time to time, she would pick up Skip, our first son, to take him home with her to spend the night or the weekend.

Late one cold, rainy evening, Mother came by to pick up Skip on her way home. Because of construction at the airfield, it was necessary to detour between two buildings at the airfield headquarters. Skip, who was four years old at the time, always stood in the seat next to my mother.

As they maneuvered along the detour in the rain, Skip said, "Grandmother, what does 'halt' mean?"

His grandmother replied, "Why, it means to stop. Why do you ask?"

Skip said, "That's what the soldier with the gun said when we drove past him."

At this point, I would like to offer some sincere thanks to the soldier who did not fire his weapon that night and let an elderly lady and a little boy go by safely.

*It's not who you are or where you've been;*
*it's where you're going that counts.*
– CAL FARLEY

# I HAD THE RIGHT OF WAY

M**Y MOTHER WORKED AT A DRY-GOODS STORE IN TOWN** for fifteen years, and she drove to and from the ranch each day on the same route.

In 1941, Camp Hood was established just outside of Killeen. The military reservation occupied about 160,000 acres of farm and ranch land. Our ranch was not included in the land occupied by the military camp at this time, but the ranch was just outside the eastern camp boundary. This location required my mother to drive across a portion of the reservation.

In time, the military built a small airport adjacent to the road that Mother traveled on the way to and from work. Mother had to drive across the taxi strip – the small road leading from the hangars to the actual runway by the small planes. All the planes using this facility were small observation planes used in maneuvers on the reservation.

On one occasion, a plane was on the taxi strip heading toward the runway at the same time my mother was driving to work. She did not stop. The plane *could not* stop in time to avoid a collision. So, they collided. Luckily, no one was hurt.

When the pilot asked, "Why didn't you stop? You could see me coming."

Mother replied, "I had the right of way!"

I knew nothing about the incident until probably six months later. An insurance company employee commented to me, "Norman, the Hartford Insurance Company has been in business some fifty years, and we have never paid for a car/airplane accident until your mother's case at Fort Hood."

*Assessment should happen constantly.*
– UNKNOWN

# SIZE 8½ D

In June of 1942, all ROTC reserve units were called from Texas A&M to active duty at Fort Sam Houston in San Antonio, Texas. When I left home from Killeen to report, I wore civilian clothes to the reception center. From there, our civilian clothes were mailed back home. Then the "real" army life began. With nothing on but olive-drab shorts, we formed a single line and paraded through the quartermaster building to receive our uniforms. It did not take very long, as no measurements were taken. They used the "eyeball" method. As we passed different stations, someone looked at each person and yelled out his "expert" opinion as to the size necessary to clothe the individual. One could hear multitudes of loud voices calling out such things as: "Pants 36, shirt 16–32, headdress 7½."

As I approached the shoe issue station, I observed a large man—perhaps six feet, four inches tall and weighing maybe 250 pounds with a rank of master sergeant—standing behind a counter. The counter was at least three feet wide, four feet high, and twenty feet long. As I passed, he leaned over the counter and yelled in a booming voice, "8½ D!"

I took the shoes size of 8½ D. I wore them on my day-to-day activities. I wore them during parades. I wore them on forced nine-mile marches. I disembarked from gliders with my 8½ D shoes.

After being discharged from the army, I continued to wear size 8½ D shoes. I continued this practice for over thirty years. Finally, I was buying a pair of boots and the salesman measured my foot. "Why are you wearing a size 8½ D?" he asked. "You should be wearing a size 10 C."

I explained to him that years before, this huge master sergeant had told me and everyone else around that my size shoe was 8½ D. That sergeant had called out the size with such authority that I had not dared to question his judgment.

I must admit that the difference between an 8½ D and a 10 C was enormous, and it might explain why wearing boots of any kind had been such a painful experience for me. At times, I thought my skin was being pulled completely away from my toenails. I had long suffered with ingrown toenails. On my left foot, I had one toe that stayed halfway under the adjoining nail.

The "eyeball" method of assigning a shoe size did not work too well for me.

*It was impossible to get a conversation going;*
*everybody was talking too much.*
– YOGI BERRA

# THE VANISHING WIFE

WHILE SERVING IN THE ARMY DURING WORLD WAR II, I was transferred from Camp Maxie, Texas, to Fort Lewis, Washington. I was allowed to drive my car and was given seven days before I had to report.

The time allowed for a visit to the countryside with Billye, so we made the trip. We went by Carlsbad Caverns in New Mexico and headed to Yellowstone National Park in Wyoming. During the war, gasoline was rationed. As a result, civilian travel was so restricted that there was not a lot of traffic in many areas of the nation.

We entered the park through the unmanned entrance on the south side. I had intended to get gas for the last several miles but had not taken the time to do so. During this time, travel was limited to mostly soldiers or sailors on leave who were also traveling through the park. As we drove farther into the park, we ran out of gas. I had noticed on the park map that the small town of Thumb was eight miles up the road. I caught a ride to Thumb, only to find that the one gas station in the village was out of business. I proceeded on to the park headquarters, which was another thirty-two miles away, and was able to catch a ride.

I had left Billye in the car as I started on my quest for gas. My time away from the car was rapidly increasing, and I grew concerned about her being alone in the car with little or no traffic on the road. Upon finally returning to the car with my ride, we observed a mother bear and two cubs around the car. The driver of my ride honked the horn several times, and the bears retreated some distance away from the car.

I approached the car only to find Billye missing. The doors were locked, but there was no Billye! As I tried to open the doors, I heard a noise inside the trunk of the car – a 1948 Plymouth coupe with only two doors and a single row of seats. The car had a door located behind the passenger seat that allowed access to the trunk from inside the car. The door was wide enough so luggage could be placed in the car using that door. Billye had locked the doors, put her seat down, and crawled into the trunk for safety when the bears surrounded the car.

Billye explained to me that she had never seen a bear other than the ones at the San Antonio Zoo. She became extremely alarmed to see the three bears approaching the car. The bears had come up to the car, placed their heads against the door's glass window, and climbed on the hood and the trunk of the car. Because she was very afraid and alone, she crawled into the trunk for safety.

This was quite an experience for Billye. She insisted that it was all my fault for not buying gas earlier in the day.

I have not run out of gas since.

*Even Napoleon had his Watergate.*
– YOGI BERRA

# THE BARN DORMITORY

WHILE OPERATING THE BEAR CREEK RANCH IN THE Hill Country near Cleo, Texas, we noticed an obscure pathway that ran through the ranch from north to south across the ranch. We found small campfire sites, empty bean and tomato cans tossed by the wayside, and areas where individuals had bedded down. These were all signs that this was a path traveled by "wetbacks," as they were called. They had crossed the Rio Grande River and were moving north to find employment.

The number of individuals making this trip captured our attention. As newcomers to this part of the Hill Country, we inquired for details. Coffee shop and feed store talk explained the situation. Several miles to the north, a rancher had built a barn with a large basement he had converted into a living area with rooms, a lounge area, and a kitchen. His purpose was to provide a place for "wetbacks" to stay until they were employed on nearby ranches or farms. In this part of the Hill Country, ranchers and farmers knew they could secure laborers from the Barn Dormitory.

We never saw the barn, but for the fifteen years we operated Bear Creek Ranch, the barn business flourished.

*You are never strong enough that you don't need help.*
– CESAR CHAVEZ

# THE RED BOOTS

DURING THE 1980S AND 1990S, OUR FAMILY OWNED A cattle and goat ranch near the village of Cleo, Texas, in the western Hill Country. Skip, our older son, lived on and operated the ranch.

It was not uncommon to find evidence that Mexicans who were illegally in the United States had crossed the ranch. Some of the evidence involved finding locations where campfires had been built and discarded empty bean cans or peach cans. Many times, when we took an overnight camping trip into the ranch, it was evident that we were being watched as we sat around our campfire. Upon closer examination, we could make out a face and eyes in the surrounding brush or timbers. The Mexicans were there because they wanted something to eat. Many times, we would pitch canned fruit, meat, and beans into their hiding place. We would not see or hear from them again for the rest of our trip.

On one occasion, Skip was in his pickup driving in

and out of the brush and timbers, searching for missing livestock. One section of the pasture was not accessible by pickup, so he began walking along a game trail. As he approached a small clearing, he saw a pair of new red cowboy boots. Alongside the boots, he saw on a rock a bar of soap that still had bubbles covering it, which indicated that it had been used very recently. Also, a pair of expensive blue jeans as well as a shirt were nearby. Skip's thought was that he had startled an individual who had taken refuge in the brush nearby, so he just returned to his pickup.

This incident is not the end of the story. Four days later, he returned to the same place. He discovered the same items were in the same spot and undisturbed. He returned home still not understanding what he had witnessed. A few days later, he took his mother to the spot. All the items were as they had been earlier on the other encounters. After a while, his mother determined that all the clothes belonged to a woman because of their small sizes.

After this, Skip asked the sheriff to come view the scene. A small canyon or ravine was near the location where the clothing had been found. The sheriff thought that possibly foul play had occurred. He also knew the area was infested with rattlesnakes and copperheads, which made him think that perhaps the person had disturbed a snake and been bitten. They searched the bottom of the canyon, but no body parts were ever found. Six months after Skip first saw the red boots, we still had no answers. It was determined that if a body had fallen or had been thrown into the canyon, wild animals would most likely have scattered any bones that might have remained.

We never did solve the mystery of the red boots.

*We must be ready to dare all for our country.*
*For history does not long entrust the care of*
*freedom to the weak or the timid.*
– DWIGHT D. EISENHOWER

# OLD BUS WITH A MESSAGE BOARD

ON BEAR CREEK RANCH, THERE WAS AN OLD, ABANDONED Greyhound bus nestled in the tree-covered hills. Years earlier after the bus had been retired, a group of deer hunters purchased it to use as a hunting cabin. They had rearranged the interior to accommodate a group of several hunters.

The bus was used for many years before it breathed its last breath. It had been left on the ranch and never moved. In time, many of the windows were broken, the door went missing, and small trees and brush had grown around it. Mexican nationals who were traveling hidden trails from the Rio Grande River to the interior of west Texas had discovered the bus. They had spread sand on the floor of the bus and added a small wood-burning stove on the sand.

Shortly after we purchased the ranch, we noticed a piece of old blackboard had been attached to the side of the interior of the bus. Later we saw messages left on the board by the Mexicans traveling through the ranch. The messages told the others who the friendly ranchers were, which ranches to avoid, and also where to seek employment.

We observed the bus and the message board for at least a dozen years. The thing that remained a mystery to us was the reason for using colored chalk to make some sentences. We knew it had some significance because it was used often during the twelve-year period.

During this time, we never saw anyone in the bus. However, there was much evidence pointing to its use. We found empty bean cans and peach cans. We observed ashes in the stove and used blankets on the bunk beds in the bus.

There was never any evidence of abuse to the ranch. No cattle or goats were ever butchered for food, and no damage was ever done to the fences. Evidently, the bus served as a way station for the Mexicans as they found their way into Texas.

*Those who deny freedom to others deserve it not for themselves.*
– ABRAHAM LINCOLN

# ONE SIZE MAY FIT MANY

BACK IN THE LATE 1920S AND 1930S, AND EVEN INTO THE 1940s, it was uncommon for people to go to an eye doctor. In fact, very few small towns even had an optometrist.

As my dad advanced in years, he needed reading glasses. It was the common practice in those days to go to Temple, a much larger community that was about thirty miles away, to shop for glasses at the Woolworth Company Store.

In Woolworth's, they had a table with four-inch high sides filled with a pile of a few hundred pairs of glasses. The procedure was to stand at the table, trying on one pair of glasses after another until a pair was found that would fit your needs.

As time passed and the glasses no longer fit your "seeing needs," it was back to the table at Woolworth's to choose glasses from the pile.

Even though my dad was an avid reader who wore reading glasses for more than forty years and lived to be over ninety years old, I don't think he ever went to an optometrist.

*There are an estimated 878 million people around the world. Nearly half of them are unemployed and live on less than $1.25 per day.*
– THE ROTARY FOUNDATION

# "STILL TRYING TO GET EVEN!"

In my childhood, neighbors were few and far between. Finding a babysitter was sometimes a problem. However, at times this problem was solved by a pooling of resources.

An aunt of mine and her three daughters lived three miles away. One daughter, Jean, was my age. Often, my mother and aunt attended the home demonstration meetings together, and I was left with my aunt's three daughters.

On one occasion, another aunt, Molly, was visiting in the home of the three daughters. This aunt had never had children. As the day continued, we kids grew tired and began to fuss about one thing or another. During one episode, I hit Jean, and she began to cry. Aunt Molly decided I needed a spanking. There were thousands of green cotton stalks in the field around the house. But no, Jean got a switch from the only mesquite tree within two miles. Limbs from mesquite trees are often twelve to eighteen or more inches long and have long green leaves and sharp thorns that can be as much as an inch in length.

Since Aunt Molly had no children, this was a new experience for her. She had the switch, and Jean encouraged her to proceed. So, she administered the spanking. I imagine few people know how effectively a two-foot-long mesquite switch with thorns can improve a six-year-old boy's behavior. When she was done, I told Jean that I would never forgive her.

But time heals all wounds. Jean is ninety-one years of age. At this writing, she lives in an assisted-living home thirty miles from my home. On her birthday, I sent her a large bouquet of flowers with six green mesquite branches mixed in with the flowers. My note read, "Still trying to get even!"

*Nobuddy ever fergits where he buried a hatchet.*
– KIN HUBBARD

# DEER HUNTING EXPOSED

In many family situations in central and west Texas, fathers consider it their obligation to train their sons to be deer hunters. So, from about age eight on, fathers take their sons deer hunting as a phase of growing up.

Our younger son, Charlie, assumed this "God-given" responsibility with his two sons. The process worked fine with Caleb, his older son; however, it was a different story with the younger son, Nathan.

Early one cold December morning, Charlie and Nathan sat in a deer blind, waiting for daylight in hopes of sighting a male deer. As the daylight seemed to be taking its time in coming, Nathan said, "Dad, can't we find something else to do that is fun?"

Stunned, Charlie said, "Why, Nathan? Don't you enjoy deer hunting?"

Nathan replied, "Well, other than having to get up so early, be still so long, sit out in the cold for hours, and be quiet so long, I guess I enjoy it."

That experience ended Nathan's training period for deer hunting. I am not sure Charlie has ever gotten over the shock.

*Creativity and innovation coming together is the beginning of change.*
– UNKNOWN

# THE LIZARD AND ROMANCE

WHEN CHARLIE WAS A TEENAGER, HE FOUND A MOUNTAIN boomer chameleon lizard on the ranch. He was absolutely fascinated with its ability to change color. He kept it in a jar with holes punched in the lid for ventilation.

When his mother made a trip to town, he went with her so he could show his prized possession to his friends. During the trip home, Charlie's mother told him not to let the lizard out of the jar. These were wasted words – the lid was already off so Charlie's two friends could get a better look. Needless to say, the lizard escaped in the car.

His mother was horrified! She slowed the car and told the boys to open all the doors. She was hoping the lizard would escape from the moving car. Still feeling insecure about the lizard's location, she decided to search the car at a nearby service station. The attendant helped with the search, but to no avail. The group agreed that the lizard had probably escaped during the open-doors event. (I was told later by the station attendant that it was quite a sight seeing a car with all four doors open approaching the station.)

That night, Skip had a date and was using the car. He and his date went to a drive-in movie, and Skip's date was sitting close to him during the movie. When she looked over at the passenger seat, she saw the lizard sitting on the back of the seat, changing colors as the light reflected from the movie screen. She screamed and began to cry loudly as she jumped out of the car. All this commotion attracted the attention of the manager of the drive-in and two policemen.

After all the disturbance calmed down and explanations were made, everything went back to normal. But Skip's date refused to return to the car and caught a ride home with someone else.

Charlie was blamed for breaking up what could have been a budding romance.

*I'm not going to buy my kids an encyclopedia.*
*Let them walk to school like I did.*
– YOGI BERRA

# TELLTALE GRADES

I ALWAYS SAY, "ONE OF OUR SONS CRAMMED FOUR YEARS of college into six years." He enjoyed college, especially the extracurricular activities. His report cards would be mailed home with failing grades. His explanation was always, "It's okay, Dad. They are going to offer the same course again next semester."

His mother would become upset and really take him to task about his failing grades. I tried to have a positive attitude about the situation. I would tell his mother, "One good thing is that you can tell by his grades that he doesn't cheat."

*There is a tendency to overestimate the quality of management talent by relying on track records.*
– UNKNOWN

# DOUBLE SPEEDING

WHEN BILLYE AND I ENTERED OUR RETIREMENT YEARS, we moved to Lake McQueeney, Texas, which is located about halfway between New Braunfels and Seguin. Lake McQueeney is a peaceful community. The only noise to break the silence is the boats and Wave Runners on the lake during the spring and summer months.

We lived on a winding road on the lake that was lined with numerous trees. The only convenience store was a half mile away on the farm-to-market road, route 725. I often went to the store without my driver's license because the road was seldom, if ever, patrolled.

One time as I drove the winding road, a highway patrolman stopped me. When he asked to see my driver's license, I explained that I only lived a few houses around the corner and did not have it with me. I volunteered to return home and pick up the license and return to where the patrolman had set up his operations. Permission was given for me to return home for the license. Upon my return to the policeman's location, he examined the license and said, "I am giving you a ticket for speeding."

I replied, "Speeding? I thought you were checking for driver's licenses."

The officer replied, "You were not only speeding when you drove up the first time, but you were speeding when you returned with your license."

I hung my head and graciously accepted the ticket.

*When you make a mistake, and you will, own up to it and learn from it. Odds are high that you will repeat it.*
– UNKNOWN

# A PLASTIC PADDLE AND
# THE WATERFALL

DURING THE EARLY 1980S, WE PURCHASED A LAKESIDE lot with a small fishing cabin on Lake McQueeney, Texas. It served our purpose for weekend trips of fishing and watersports.

In time, we built a boathouse and purchased a motorboat. I took great pleasure in taking the boat for a trip late in the afternoon. I enjoyed going to the dam where a ski lodge was located. I did not always stop at the lodge but proceeded to make a circle in front of the dam. Sometimes I would go dangerously close to the dam's edge where water flowed over it.

Upon one occasion, with darkness approaching, I made my usual run in, and I went close to the dam as usual, but this time, the boat motor sputtered, ran, sputtered again—and died. I was near where the flow of the water picked up speed before going over the dam. I frantically began searching the boat for a paddle. I only found a plastic paddle. This was an eighteen-foot motorboat with a mind of its own. As I worked with the plastic paddle, it would bend slightly, which forced me to turn the paddle over and paddle with the other side.

The boat was caught in the lake flow areas between the slow-moving current before it reached the accelerated area of flow toward the dam. I desperately paddled to stay in the somewhat-calm area of flow. In fact, I paddled for nearly half an hour in a panicked effort to move toward shore and at the same time keep from going over the dam. I finally succeeded in reaching the shore, only to find high banks at the water's edge. Using the tree limbs that overhung the water's edge, I pulled the boat back from the dam area until I reached calm waters. I found a family's boat dock area, secured the boat, and walked up a flight of stairs leading to someone's backyard.

I entered the backyard, and within seconds I heard a loud, vicious bark. The largest, ugliest dog I had ever seen was running full speed toward me. Normally, I can't jump a five-foot fence, but that day—I had no trouble clearing it. I walked to the main road and called my wife to bring me some gasoline for the boat.

You may not believe it, but I have not taken the boat on that trip down to the dam since that night long ago.

*Victory is the prize. Pain is the price.*
– COACH PAUL "BEAR" BRYANT

# NEVER SAY NOAH AGAIN

LIFE ON LAKE MCQUEENEY CAN BRING UNWANTED thrills and excitement. The lake is located on the Guadalupe River between New Braunfels and Seguin, Texas. There are five small lakes located one right after the other. The first lake in the chain is Lake Dunlap, which is about twenty miles below Canyon Lake, one of the larger lakes in Texas. Canyon Lake was designed to control flooding on the Guadalupe River. Canyon Lake's design does this very well – except when a large amount of rainfall occurs beyond the dam site.

Such was the occasion in July of 1998, when twenty-two inches of rain fell over thirty hours. We lived lakeside on Lake McQueeney, the second lake in the chain of five.

Other than word of mouth, radio, and television, there was no flood-warning system at this time. Periodically, someone from above the lake would call some acquaintance and report high water in their area, and word would be passed on.

During that July afternoon, water began overflowing the lake's banks, and it began a slow climb toward our home. By 5:00 p.m., the water was rising quickly. Billye expressed concern, to which I nonchalantly commented, "We are not going to have water in the house. Cool it, Noah."

But by seven o'clock, I decided to move our two cars. We each moved a car to the highest ground in the area. When I took Billye back to the house, she had to wade in water to get to our front door. I returned the second car to the higher ground and began my walk to the nearest street to our house. I had to swim to the house. (I really didn't want to return, but I thought Billye would take a dim view of my actions if I didn't.)

Eighteen-wheel trucks, boats, and helicopters were used to rescue people. However, when the neighbors saw us leave in the two cars, they thought we were leaving to find shelter. No one came after us, so we spent the night on the second floor of our home. We watched the water climb up the stairs.

On more than one occasion that long night, Billye made a pointed comment: "Noah, I believe the water is going to get into the house."

At about ten thirty-five that night, the radio announcer informed us the floodwater had crested. The water was then about six inches from the second floor. By morning, the water receded to only four feet in the house. The next day, the cleanup started.

My reference to Noah was a poor choice. Not only did I hear it a number of times the night of the flood, but even now, when Billye gets upset with me over something, a reference to Noah is repeated even though it has been fourteen years since the flood.

*Challenge your assumptions frequently.*
– UNKNOWN

# LEARNING TO SPEND MONEY

IN THE EARLY YEARS OF OUR MARRIAGE, WE WERE friends with another couple who were somewhat older than we were. The man had inherited a considerable amount of wealth. He had married a girl from a small farming community, and she had a sheltered and religious background.

We were all spending a Saturday afternoon at a shopping center, and we split up. The ladies went in one direction, and the men went in another. Later in the afternoon, we met at an agreed-upon spot. When the ladies arrived, the friend told her husband that she found a dress she had fallen in love with. Her husband said, "Well, let's see it."

She replied, "I think I should wait until it goes on sale."

The man replied, "Helen, you must learn how to spend money! You don't need to wait until something goes on sale! If you like it and want it, go ahead and buy it!"

My wife must have thought he was talking to her because she really took the statement to heart. She has definitely been practicing that philosophy ever since: if you like it and want it, buy it!

*Money is not free.*
– FINKELSTEIN

# FOOTLOCKERS TO
# THE RESTROOM

Skip, our older son, enrolled in Texas A&M as a freshman, I think mainly to please me. At any rate, he was in the Cadet Corps and went through all of the traditions as well as the hazing, which has always been a big part of A&M life.

His tolerance was tested to the limit one time when his cadet company did something that was unforgivable according to the upperclassmen. As a punishment, all freshmen were to undress in their rooms from 6:00 p.m. to 6:00 a.m. They could only wear their raincoats. Each floor of the dorm had only two gang restrooms that were located at each end of the floor. As further punishment, a freshman had to carry his footlocker back and forth to the restroom with him every time he went.

This procedure was to last a full week. As one might

guess, this activity made a lasting impression on each freshman, especially on Skip who did not return to A&M after his freshman year.

*The multitude who require to be led still hate their leaders.*
– WILLIAM HAZLITT

# CHARLIE AND THE GYM WALL

WHEN CHARLIE WAS IN SIXTH GRADE, HIS TEACHER SENT another boy and him outside the school building with the assignment to spray paint a sign on a two-by-three-foot poster board.

When the sign was finished, they discovered they still had paint in the spray can. What they should do with the extra paint was their dilemma. Their solution was to paint a three-foot high sign on the gym wall that read: "Seniors 1971." The school gym was about three blocks from the county courthouse, and on a clear day, one could easily read the sign while standing on the courthouse steps.

The principal called me to inform me of the situation. I suggested that he administer a paddling to Charlie, which he did not do.

This situation created a dilemma for me because of the number of people who were bound to ask about the sign painted on the gym. Their answer would be something like "Yes, the superintendent's son did that!" I knew this would not be good public relations.

That afternoon, when I arrived home, Charlie met me at the door with my belt in his hand. The gym wall was made from white limestone rocks with a rough surface. Charlie and I spent several hours on two different Saturdays removing his work of art from the gym wall. This ended Charlie's painting career.

*High school dropouts are four times as likely to be unemployed as those who have completed four or more years of college.*
– UNKNOWN

# ON MY KNEES IN THE BAR DITCH

During the late 1960s and early 1970s, we lived on a ranch seven miles south of Killeen. We had a family car as well as a red-and-white Ford pickup that we used in the ranch operations.

When our older son, Skip, was a junior in high school, we began letting him use the family car for dates. On one occasion when he returned the car, he had driven seventy-two miles. I thought this was excessive and grounded him for three months.

He had taken the grounding in good style, and later on a Wednesday, he asked if he might use the car for a date on the next Saturday night. I agreed.

I usually went into town on Saturday around noon and returned by five thirty or six o'clock. On this occasion, I was involved in a golf game and lost track of time. Around six thirty, I realized I had overstayed my trip to town and was concerned about making Skip late for his date. I rushed to the car and started to return to the ranch.

I was almost to the ranch when a red-and-white pickup passed me. I thought, *That must be Skip. I am late. He gave up on me and is going on his date in the old ranch truck.* I turned around to follow him, thinking we could exchange vehicles. It was then that I realized the speed he was driving. At one point on the country road, I reached eighty-two miles per hour. By then, I was extremely angry, first because of the dangerous speed he was driving and second for his lack of concern for family property.

I finally caught up with him when he stopped at the red light before entering the highway. When the light changed, the red-and-white pickup entered the highway. I pulled alongside the pickup and forced it into the bar ditch. I got out of my car, rushed to the pickup, jerked the door open, and in a loud voice, I said, "Skip! Get out of that truck!"

Skip did not get out of the pickup. The person who got out was at least six feet tall and weighed some 240 pounds. If history had recorded this scene, it would have recorded a grown man on his knees in a bar ditch trying to convince a huge man that he thought he was his son driving a red-and-white truck.

It turned out that the huge man was a rancher who had recently purchased a ranch several miles down the road. I explained what had happened, and he laughed. I could not laugh with him because I was still shaking.

Skip did make his date in the family car. This time, I did not check the mileage when he returned.

*Little League baseball is a very good thing because*
*it keeps the parents off the streets.*
– YOGI BERRA

# A BEGINNING RANCHER

In 1960, we purchased a ranch south of Killeen with the intention of raising cattle. It had been twenty-one years since I had lived on a ranch, and I had a lot to learn about this endeavor!

As it turned out, my job kept me occupied in town every day except Sunday, so Skip became the rancher. He was a freshman in high school but eager to learn the ranching business. We were fortunate that Cy Waters, the rancher next door, was a kindly fellow and over years became an excellent teacher and a true friend for Skip.

As an example, Skip's first calf was stillborn which proved to be quite a blow for the young rancher. Cy Waters took Skip to the sales barn in Temple where they purchased a two-day-old calf. They returned to the ranch, and Cy skinned the dead calf and tied the skin on the calf they had just purchased. The new calf was hungry and eager to nurse. As the new calf approached the mother cow who had lost her calf, she smelled the calf's skin and allowed it to nurse. By having the skin of the lost calf on it, the new calf had the scent of her calf, and she accepted the calf as her own and raised it until it was weaned. Skip learned this was a common practice among ranchers.

Until Skip left for college, he and Cy spent many hours together. They were a team. Together they sprayed cattle, mixed feed, branded calves, vaccinated all the livestock, and marketed animals to be taken from the herd.

Cy must have been sixty years of age when he and Skip met. After Skip went to college, we sold the ranch and moved away from the Killeen area. In so doing, over a period of time we lost contact with Cy.

Some twenty-five years later, we heard Cy had passed away. Skip did not know where Cy was buried, so he began a search of north Texas cemeteries to find his grave. Skip wanted to make sure that Cy had a tombstone and a properly marked grave.

After weeks of searching, he found the grave. It had a tombstone and was properly marked.

Skip could rest easy now and cherish the memories of Cy and him ranching together.

*Planning, coaching, and preparation are essential to success.*
– UNKNOWN

# A SHOE IN THE MUD

WE HAD JUST MOVED TO THE RANCH WHICH WAS SEVEN miles from town. The ranch house was another three hundred yards off the all-weather county road. This move was never sanctioned by Billye. The family vote to move was three to one: the three being the boys in the family and the one being Billye. Our usual method of family operation was that the boys left for school each morning and Billye went into town from time to time for meetings and to shop.

Caliche gravel makes an excellent road base once it becomes wet and is allowed to dry. Billye had gone to town early one morning, and during her stay, it rained about three inches. Upon her return to the ranch, the caliche was soft and far from becoming a hard surface.

I received a phone call at work saying that the car was stuck in the caliche some distance from the house. I drove to the ranch looking for Billye's car by staying on the old gravel road. Her car was stuck up to the axle. As I walked on to the house on the caliche road, I first found a loaf of bread. I assumed it had fallen out of the grocery sack. Next I found a can of beans, a box of cereal, and finally a lady's shoe that was stuck deep in the mud. At this point, I realized that the incident was no longer funny. I was in deep trouble.

The caliche road bed did dry and become a solid road bed—however, not before I received an extended period of the silent treatment.

*A man is not a man until he has a woman to tell him what to do.*
– DEMARIO

# SO FAR OUT

Skip, our older son, was attempting to tell a new friend where he lived. He said it was on a ranch and tried to tell him which road and where he needed to turn, etc.

Finally, he said, "We live so far out in the country that we have to come back toward town to hunt."

*The can opener was invented forty-eight years after the can.*
– UNKNOWN

# OUT THE DOOR WITH
# MY HANDS UP

LIVING ON A RANCH SEVEN MILES FROM TOWN NORMALLY provides peace and quiet on a regular basis. However, there are times and circumstances when the norm is placed aside. This can be especially true when there is an army post located twelve miles away.

Fort Hood maintained a large stockade with a full complement of inmates. On one occasion, our night on the ranch was disturbed by sounds of commotion, speeding vehicles, and two large searchlights beaming into a forest about two hundred yards from the ranch house. The activities lasted until two o'clock in the morning. We had no explanation as to what was going on.

The next morning, all the activities had ceased. Things seemed to return to normal. However, upon arriving in town, the conversation was buzzing about the escape of the five inmates from the Fort Hood stockade. The escapees had been tracked to a ranch on Stagecoach Road. Hence, the noise and commotion during the night.

After Billye completed her shopping in town that day, she came by my office and insisted that I go home with her to check the house for intruders. She was concerned that the escapees might be hiding in or near our ranch house.

We drove into the driveway of the ranch house where Billye stayed in the car while I proceeded to go in and check the house for possible intruders. I checked each room, all the closets, and under all the beds. I found nothing. I decided to add extra drama to the situation by walking out of the house with my hands up in the air. I wanted it to appear that someone was holding a gun to my back.

Billye had turned the car around so that it was heading out of the driveway and pointing toward the road leaving the ranch. When she saw me come out with my hands in the air, she took off in a cloud of dust, leaving me to face the would-be escapees on my own. Within a period of about thirty minutes, I saw a carload of military MPs, a sheriff's car, and Billye entering the ranch gate.

I was embarrassed to confess what I had done, and I was definitely the only one in the group to appreciate the humor in the situation!

*Don't look back. Something might be gaining on you.*
– SATCHEL PAIGE

# MOST OF IT WAS YOUR FAULT

BILLYE AND I SPENT MANY HAPPY YEARS OF MARRIED LIFE together. One time, I commented that we had experienced some hard times during our time together, to which she replied, "Yes, and most of it has been your fault!"

*Successful marriage is an art that can only be learned with difficulty.*
*But it gives pride and satisfaction, like any other expertness that is*
*hard won....I would say that the surest measures of a man's or woman's*
*maturity is the harmony, style, joy, dignity he creates in his marriage,*
*and the pleasure and inspiration he provides for his spouse. An immature*
*person may achieve great success in a career but never in marriage.*
– BENJAMIN SPOCK

# UNHAND ME, YOU BRUTE

During the early years of our marriage, we had one son, Skip. Thanks to my job in the public school and being a hometown couple, we had a number of close friends. Two single young men, Bill Alford and Bob Taylor, visited our home often. Skip was eighteen months old and had learned to talk, so Bill and Bob got a kick out of teasing and playing with him.

Since they enjoyed teasing Skip, I taught him to say, "Unhand me, you brute" when they picked him up and were scuffling with him. This was all well and good, and all of us got a kick out of the horseplay.

However, we were not prepared for the incident that took place at Skipper's christening. When the day arrived, Billye, Skip, and I were sitting on the front row of the First Methodist Church in Killeen, Texas.

As the service progressed, the minister called us to come forward. As is custom, after a few words relating to christening, he reached out and took Skip from his mother's arms—to which Skip said in a loud, clear voice, "Unhand me, you brute!"

The congregation roared in laughter. Billye turned beet red. I wanted to fall through the floor. After the initial shock, the minister joined in the laughter.

The christening then proceeded in a lighthearted, happy mood.

*There are only two lasting bequests we can hope to give our children, one of those is roots; the other is wings.*
– WILLIAM HODDING CASTER, JR.

# DON'T FORGET SANTA CLAUS

When Skip was growing up, it was customary during church service to have the young children come to the front of the church so that the pastor could offer a brief lesson about the Bible.

I remember one occasion when the pastor asked if the young children could name some of the men mentioned in the Bible. Several individuals spoke up, naming Jesus, Moses, Paul, Job, and Abraham. Skip, who was five years old, said with a tone of authority, "Don't forget Santa Claus!"

*It was tomorrow yesterday.*
– UNKNOWN

# A PESSIMISTIC ATTITUDE

A PESSIMISTIC ATTITUDE CAN GROW ON A PERSON, OFTEN without him even realizing it. I fall into that category from time to time.

Our younger son crammed four years of college into six years. At times when he would fail a college course and I would express my concern for the cost or even his lack of effort, his reply was, "It's all right, Dad. I will take the course again next semester."

From time to time, people would ask, "What will Charlie be when he finishes college?"

Without much thought, my answer was, "About thirty-two, I think."

*The secret to getting ahead is getting started.*
– MARK TWAIN

# LOST SPEAKER FEES

As I grew in my profession as a school administrator, I sought opportunities to improve my public-speaking skills. While living in Lampasas, Texas, I was provided with the chance to participate in a Dale Carnegie class called "How to Win Friends and Influence People." This course was mainly offered to local bank personnel, but upon my completion of it, I found it helped to open many professional doors for me during the following years.

In time, I had the opportunity to make speeches to education groups and service clubs. The fee for the first speeches started at twenty-five dollars. Later on, the fees increased to fifty dollars, and in a few years, it went up to one hundred dollars per speech.

When Charlie, our younger son, was a junior in high school, I thought it would be a good opportunity to give him some financial training. So, one night I informed him that I was being paid for some of the speaking engagements. I proposed that I would give him the fees I received for the speeches if he would open a bank account in his name and deposit the funds into the account. Charlie's reaction was surprising to me—he declined the offer! He informed me that he wanted cash instead of checks. He wanted the funds to be readily available to him when he needed them. I withdrew my offer.

A few weeks later, Charlie approached me again about my proposal. He said he had changed his mind. He would be glad to accept the speaking fees under my conditions. I told him, "No, I made the offer, and you turned it down. I am not making the same offer again. Case closed."

It wasn't very long after this when my audiences grew, and the fees grew to $2,500 in some situations. Charlie has often lamented his decision to pass up my speaking offer. This is sometimes a topic of conversation at the dinner table on Thanksgiving and Christmas and other holidays.

*Review your decisions and efforts at regular intervals.*
– UNKNOWN

# HOMETOWN CHARM

A teenage boy living in Lampasas, Texas, during the 1960s had a charmed life at his fingertips. Charlie Hall had such an opportunity, which he took advantage of to the fullest.

He and his friends on any given day would go to the nine-hole golf course that ran along Sulphur Creek. In their golf bags were the usual golf clubs plus a fishing pole. The normal plan of operation was to play the course holes one through four then switch from golf to fishing along the creek that bordered holes five, six, and seven. When they reached holes eight and nine, they continued the golf game.

This was the procedure which might take the majority of an entire day or as many hours as they cared to devote to the activity. This was part of the charm of living on the edge of the Hill Country in a town called Lampasas.

*Together, we have experienced life.*
*Separately, we will pursue our dreams.*
*Forever, our memories will remain.*
– UNKNOWN

# GRAY MOSS INN

In the rural area some twenty miles north of San Antonio, Texas, there is a famous restaurant. They advertise that General Robert E. Lee of Civil War fame once dined there, also Babe Ruth, as well as General Dwight Eisenhower, and a number of movie stars.

Because of its fame and notoriety, Billye decided she wanted us to have dinner there. We arrived early in the evening, but the surrounding area was not what we expected. There were many large trees that were covered in low-hanging moss. We discovered that there was no paved parking and no fence or sidewalk leading to the front door. The building looked as though it had been a home that had been converted into a place of business.

Billye did not want to go in. She said, "Let's go someplace else for dinner."

I said, "No, you have wanted to come here for a long time. So, let's go in."

Her thinking was reinforced by the car parked right

beside us. There was a man standing outside the passenger side of his car insisting that his wife get out and go in.

We passed through the outside bar area which was filled with hippie-dressed individuals who were drinking, dancing, and talking loudly. As we entered the dining area, we were greeted by an elderly lady, who seated us in one of the several secluded areas. Our waitress was also dressed like a hippie but was very nice and pleasant.

The very interesting thing about this dining experience was that Billye became concerned about our safety. She took off her jewelry, placed it in a jewelry pouch in her purse, and sat on the purse the remainder of the evening.

I never asked what the safety features of this activity might be; however, Billye never asked me to take her to Gray Moss Inn again.

*Past success is no guarantee of future success.*
– UNKNOWN

# A LESSON TOO LATE

WHEN BILLYE WAS THIRTY-EIGHT YEARS OLD, SHE WAS given the opportunity to have a golf lesson from Harvey Penick, who had quite a reputation for teaching some of the top male golfers like Tom Kite and Ben Crenshaw. Rumor was that he taught and coached professional ladies' golf but seldom spent time with amateurs. However, over a period of time, Billye's friends persuaded him to give Billye a golf lesson.

On the morning of the first lesson, Mr. Penick had her get into the golf cart with him. He drove her to the practice course at Austin Country Club. According to Billye, they drove up to a practice tee box. Mr. Penick did not get out of the cart, but he pitched five golf balls on the tee box and told her he wanted to see her hit the balls. Billye was somewhat nervous, but she teed up the first ball, took her time, and hit the ball down the fairway for a long distance. She then teed up the second ball and again hit a shot straight down the fairway for an even better distance.

At this point, Mr. Penick asked, "Have you ever hit a ball that far before?" to which Billye replied, "Yes, sir, that is about my average distance." At this point, the golf lesson seemed to take on a new meaning to him. He got out of the cart and gave Billye a number of meaningful golf tips.

Mr. Penick gave Billye five golf lessons. At the end of the fifth lesson, she received the best compliment concerning her athletic ability that she had ever had. Harvey Penick looked at Billye and smiled. He told her, "If you were twenty years younger and I was forty years younger, I would take you on the PGA Women's Golf Tour." This was a super compliment to Billye that she cherished forever.

*Whether you think you can or can't, you're right.*
– RANDY PAUSCH

# THE RESTROOM AT
# THE FIRE STATION

Our younger son, Charlie, started school at age six. I had been principal of Killeen's only elementary school for almost ten years and principal of a junior high school for three years. During this time, which was immediately after World War II, Killeen had a population of seven thousand people, and as a principal, I knew a large number of its citizens. Because of my connection with the community, Charlie had come in contact with an unusual number of adults.

Charlie had been fascinated by fire trucks and the fire station in Killeen for several years. Many times, on our Saturday visits to one of the fire stations, he was allowed to sit in the truck and climb from one end to the other. A large number of fire station employees, including the fire chief and fire marshal, knew him by name.

Charlie had entered first grade at Fowler Elementary

School. During the second week of school, he had permission to leave the classroom to go to the restroom.

Fire Station Number Two was located about ten blocks from the school in a residential area. He seized the opportunity to walk to the fire station. When he approached the firehouse, several of the firemen greeted him and asked why he was not in school. He explained that he had come to use the restroom. The fireman asked him if they did not have restrooms at the school. Charlie told them he did not know; he had not taken time to check into the restroom situation.

By this time, the fire marshal had appeared and became involved in questioning Charlie. Charlie was allowed to sit in the fire engine while the marshal called the elementary school. He reported Charlie's whereabouts to the principal, Harold Thomas.

I was never sure exactly what transpired during that conversation, but the fire marshal and the principal devised a plan to return Charlie to school. The marshal asked Charlie if he would like to go back to school in the marshal's red car. Charlie expressed great delight in the proposition. Just as the marshal turned into the driveway to the entrance of the school, he touched the siren, and, as prearranged, the principal stepped out from behind a column at the school entryway.

As Charlie opened the door and got out of the car, the principal said, "Hi, Charlie. Where have you been?"

Charlie replied, "I been to use the restroom."

I thought the principal was a real professional in how he handled the situation. He said nothing further to Charlie then or anytime in the future about the incident. But as you can imagine, Charlie's range of restroom use was greatly restricted from then on.

Blondy Rucker, the fire marshal, and Harold Thomas, the principal, took great delight in relating the story around town, and Charlie became known by even more people.

*You can never make a second first impression.*
– UNKNOWN

# THE HIGH DIVING BOARD

DURING THE SUMMER MONTHS, I OFTEN WORKED AT THE office during the morning and went home for lunch. Before returning to the office, I would take Charlie, our younger son, to swim at the city pool.

One day around 3:00 p.m., the pool manager called my office to instruct me to come pick Charlie up because he had used the restroom in the swimming pool. On the way back to the pool, I thought, *How do they know Charlie used the restroom in the pool? Other kids might also urinate in the pool while swimming.*

When I arrived at the pool, Charlie was sitting on a bench outside the entrance. He went to the car while I had a conference with the pool manager. My approach was the same as what I had reasoned on the drive to the pool. I said, "How do you know Charlie urinated in the pool? I imagine some of the other kids do the same thing."

The pool manager was calm and collected. In a very

deliberate voice, he replied. "Yes, that may be true for some. But Charlie did it from the high diving board."

The manager's explanation was quite specific and satisfactory. I left without any more questions, delivered Charlie home, and returned to work.

*Listening well is the best way of being heard.*
– UNKNOWN

# FIVE DOLLARS AND
# TWENTY-ONE YEARS LATER

WHEN I WAS DISCHARGED FROM THE MILITARY SERVICE in 1946, we returned to our hometown of Killeen, Texas. We started our family there, and we had many happy years in Killeen. Our two sons, Skip and Charlie, were known by the community. The town was the kind where the boys could go to the movies alone. They could shop, get haircuts, and go to and from school with very little supervision.

One time when Charlie was in third grade, as he was leaving the barbershop, he found a five-dollar bill on the sidewalk. He returned to the shop and explained about finding the bill and that he wished to return it. The barbers laughed and told Charlie to keep it. They told him there was no way of knowing who might have lost it. He told the barbers his dad would want him to return it to whoever lost it. He asked again if he could leave it with the barbers. As Charlie began to get frustrated, the barber said Charlie could take it to the police station. The police station was a few blocks away, so Charlie went there to explain his dilemma and turn in the five dollars. Again Charlie was told that the money was lost by an unknown individual, and he should keep it. Again he stated that his dad would not want him to keep the money. At length, the police chief agreed to keep the money at the station.

Twenty-one years later, when I returned to the same neighborhood barbershop, the shop owner related the story to a number of patrons and me.

This story reinforced what I have observed many times: an individual's reaction to a situation can last for a very long time.

*Character education is not old-fashioned, and it's not about bringing religion into the classroom. Character is the "X factor" that experts in parenting and education have deemed integral to success.*
– JESSICA LAHEY

# TOO MUCH INFORMATION

Skip was about twelve years old when he asked his mother about Daylight Savings Time. She told him it had something to do with giving the farmers more daylight to harvest their fields. Then she told him there might be more to it than that. "Just wait and ask your dad when he comes home."

Skip told her, "I don't want to know that much about Daylight Savings Time."

*No legacy is as great as honesty.*
– WILLIAM SHAKESPEARE

# HIT HIM AGAIN

As a superintendent of schools, you can stay in one place long enough and say no to enough people that your welcome in the community becomes questionable. I had such a position in a west Texas town for six years. Not only had I said no to enough people, but the football team had not won district during any of my years of tenure. We had replaced the football coach to no avail. So, the fault must lie with the superintendent of schools.

The majority of the school board still had a positive attitude. However, the athletic-minded individuals had become somewhat vocal and from a distance spoke out expressing discontent.

My wife and I were playing tennis one Sunday afternoon on one of the city courts. I had just started wearing contact lenses and was going through a period of adjustment. During a volley exchange, she hit a hard smash that landed at my feet. The ball bounced up and hit me in the face. As I recovered, I realized my vision was somewhat distorted. As it turned out, the contact in one eye was missing. I walked around the area trying to spot the lost contact, but to no avail.

Realizing that the contact must be somewhere close, I got down on my hands and knees and began moving around the area, searching for the missing contact. My wife continued to walk around holding her tennis racket in one hand and softly hitting the other hand into the racket strings.

I can understand what the two of us looked like to anyone passing by. It could have been perceived that she hit me and knocked me down. I was in the process of getting up when a car drove by. Someone in the car yelled in a loud voice, "Hit him again!"

*One of the most striking differences between a cat*
*and a lie is that a cat has only nine lives.*
– MARK TWAIN

# YOU WOULDN'T BELIEVE
# ME IF I TOLD YOU

WHILE I WAS SERVING AS SUPERINTENDENT OF SCHOOLS in Andrews, Texas, we lived across the street from the number-six hole of the golf course and three blocks from the club tennis courts. I was sitting in the den watching TV on a Saturday night when I suddenly discovered that I had misplaced my glasses.

I searched around inside the house with no results. Then I remembered I had taken the garbage out to the new dumpster in the alley which served eight families living in the immediate area. I reasoned that I must have dropped my glasses on the way to the alley or had dropped them as I leaned over to place the garbage inside the dumpster. So, with a flashlight, I retraced my steps to the alley, looking around my route. No glasses.

My next theory was that I had dropped them into the dumpster. Since the dumpster had just been placed in the alley the day before and I was the first to dump into it, I deduced that it was our garbage. So, I deemed it was okay for me to crawl into the dumpster and methodically remove items from different sacks, using my flashlight to check each item for any trace of my glasses. As I was finishing my search, without success, I glanced from inside the dumpster toward the alley.

There, watching every move I made, was a man I did not know. I did not care to meet him under these circumstances, but I said, "Hi." He did not say anything. I crawled from the dumpster and started walking down the alley. Our yard had a ten-foot high concrete fence around the backyard. I did not want to go into our yard because it would be a dead giveaway to the man as to who I was, so I continued down the alley. Two backyards down the alley was a fence about three feet high with a gate facing the alley. I decided to go into this yard and stay until the man watching me went on his way.

I entered the yard and started toward the back door. I had forgotten the two huge dogs my neighbor kept in the yard for protection. I had made no more than ten steps toward the house when I heard the dogs come off the back porch with loud, furious barks. I ran and jumped over the fence back into the alley. I glanced back up the alley, and, sure enough, the man was still standing there, observing my retreat.

I decided to walk down the alley to the country club. As I reached the club, I turned right, went a half block, and turned to my house, using the street separating houses on the street from the golf course.

As I entered the house and returned to the den, Billye said, "Where have you been?"

I said, "You wouldn't believe me if I told you."

The story did not end there. When I went to Sunday school the next morning, much was said about some people with responsible jobs going through the dumpsters looking for no telling what. The city council met the next Thursday night to pass a "mock" resolution prohibiting citizens from taking residence in city-owned dumpsters.

I never found out the identity of the man in the alley, but he did spread the word.

*Nobody goes there anymore. It's too crowded.*
– YOGI BERRA

# SKIPCHA

WHEN BOTH OF OUR SONS WERE STILL AT HOME, WE bought a 411-acre ranch in order to give the boys an outside interest and to direct their attention away from some of the activities of the army camp environment of Fort Hood.

The ranch was seven miles from Killeen and included varied topography. We considered several names for the ranch, and all were discarded except Skipcha. The *Skip* was for our older son, Skip, and the *Cha* was for our younger son, Charlie. The name worked really well. We placed a sign at the ranch entrance, had placemats made for use at the ranch, and painted a sign on the pickup truck.

We only lived on the ranch for three years before Skip went off to college. I took a job about thirty miles away as superintendent of schools in Lampasas, Texas. Our three years on the ranch gave us a lifetime of memories. The boys rode their horses in the annual Killeen Rodeo each night in the grand entry. We branded cattle, went on trail drives, and had cookouts on the lone mountaintop. We enjoyed many ranch-related activities.

After leaving the ranch, we continued to own and operate it for another twenty years. As time went by, we sold the ranch to a housing developer, who named the development the Skipcha Ranch. Also, the Killeen school system named one of their new elementary schools in that area Skipcha Elementary.

Without a doubt, the ranch experience was the highlight of the boys' growth years. Even today, fifty-five years later, we still relive our days on the ranch.

*Someone is sitting in the shade today because*
*someone planted a tree a long time ago.*
– WARREN BUFFETT

# TOO MANY TITLES

DURING MY DAYS ON THE RANCH, ESPECIALLY ON THE weekends, I tried to live the life of a cowboy. I dug post holes, repaired fences, doctored the livestock, and branded calves. I dressed the part of an active rancher with old cowboy boots, well-worn blue jeans, and a battered hat to match.

On one occasion, Charlie and I went to town to buy a pickup load of fence staves. Staves are small cedar posts that are placed along a fence row between the large, permanent cedar posts. We drove to the post yard and loaded about fifty staves into the old pickup truck. I had recently received my doctor of education degree, and Charlie seemed to be very proud of this. As I worked to load the staves, Charlie announced to the post-yard operators that his daddy was a doctor. Several years before, I had been on the coaching staff at the Killeen Hill School, and several of the players had grown up and still lived in Killeen. As I continued to load the staves, one of my ex-players drove by and yelled, "Hello, Coach Hall." I was also the commander of the local army reserve unit. Sure enough, the fellow delivering the Coca-Cola addressed me as Captain Hall. In addition to this, I taught a veterans' night school. One of my students came to the post yard during this time and commented to the post-yard operator that he was one of my students.

When I finished loading the pickup, I asked the post-yard operator if he would accept a check. His answer was no. "I have heard too many titles. I will only accept cash." He refused to let me use the loaded pickup to go cash a check anyplace, so I had to walk almost a mile to a convenience store on the highway to cash a check. I then returned to the post yard, paid for the staves, and made my way to the ranch. Upon my return, I explained to Billye that all those letters behind my name were not necessarily a blessing.

*We must deal with the world as it is—not as we wish it to be.*
– ROBERT GATES

# FLOODWATERS ON BEAR CREEK

SKIP, OUR OLDER SON, MOVED TO OUR SECOND RANCH near Cleo, Texas. He had operated our ranch just outside Killeen while he was still in high school until he went to college. Ranching was his first love, even while he worked and retired from another profession.

The ranch house was on high ground on the shore of Bear Creek. While talking to a neighbor, he wondered where the name Bear Creek came from. He knew that bears had never roamed that part of the state. The neighbor explained that the hills on both sides of the creek were very rocky, with little grass. When it rained two to three inches in a short period of time, the water filled up the creek, and a head rise quickly formed, causing a sheet of water sometimes three feet high to charge down the creek, endangering anything in its path.

Several weeks later, when it had rained most of the night, this same neighbor phoned Skip to tell him to go look at the creek now so that he would have a better understanding of why it was called Bear Creek. Skip did go view the creek at that time. He got down into the creek bottom, where only inches of water had accumulated. Within minutes, he heard a strange noise, only to look up and see a wall of water about three feet high coming down the creek channel. The water was kicking up sticks, debris, rocks, and anything else in its path. Skip raced to the high bank of the creek to watch the floodwater go by. Then he understood the origin of the name Bear Creek. Thus, the name he selected for the ranch was Bear Creek Ranch.

*This world is made up of those who can and those who can't.*
– UNKNOWN

# HE CAN'T COME RIGHT NOW

When Skip, our older son, was four years old, he was fascinated by the telephone. He tried to answer it every time it rang. On one occasion, his mother was working in the yard, and I was in the bathroom. At this point, the phone sounded, and since Skip had no competition in getting to the phone, he answered it.

From the bathroom, I heard this announcement: "He can't come right now. He is sitting on the commode." Needless to say, the damage was already done. At church the next Sunday, Skip's ability to give detailed information was the talk of the day. It took me weeks to get conversations to return to other topics.

*It's like deja vu all over again.*
− YOGI BERRA

# THE SEARCH IS OVER

Upon changing jobs, it was necessary for me to employ an administrative secretary. We ran ads in the local newspapers and on the Internet. The ads resulted in forty-two applicants who expressed interest in the position. The position was well paid, but I was still surprised at the volume of responses.

I methodically reviewed the qualifications of each applicant. One particularly attracted my attention. The individual was a waitress at a local Hooter's restaurant. At that time in our part of the country, the waitresses' uniforms in a Hooter's restaurant were bare chests with short shorts.

My response to my wife was, "The search is over! I have made my selection!"

To which she replied, "No! The search is not over! I will interview her; you interview the other forty-one applicants."

I never knew what happened to what I thought was the best-qualified applicant. I know she did not report to work.

*The difference between something good and something better and something great is attention to detail.*
– CHARLES R. SWINDOLL

*1925 Three Years Old*

*1942 Horse at Ranch*

*1943 A&M*

*1952 Billye*

*1988 Huffman School District*

*1979 America Association of School Administrators New Orleans*

*With Gov. & Mrs. Dolph Briscoe*
*1978 Governors Mansion*

*1974 Norman and Billye*

*1974 Norman and Billye*

*1976 Norman Hall*

*1978 American Association of School
Administrators Pontiac MI*

*1985 Beaver Creek Golf Course*

*Charlie, Norman and Skip*
*1986 Alaska Bear Hunt*

*1987 Fishing in Alaska*

*Skip, Charlie and Norman*
*1987 Old Mexico Deer Hunt*

*1987 Yosemite National Park*

*1989 Skiing Utah*

*1996 Camp Pendleton*

*1996 San Diego AASA Tournament*

*2000s Billye and Norman in McQueeney*

*2015 Billye and Norman*

*2016 Office in McQueeney*

*2017 Home and Richard Milburn Academy Office*

# Professional Stories

My professional life began in 1941 in a one-room schoolhouse. After returning from the army in 1946, I took a coaching/teaching position in my hometown of Killeen. During my tenure in the Killeen school system, I served as an elementary school principal and a secondary school principal. After that I became the superintendent of Lampasas schools in 1963. I served as superintendent for several other school districts in Texas from 1970 through the 1990s. Some of these were Andrews ISD, Round Rock ISD, and Huffman ISD. I am presently the superintendent of ten Texas charter schools. School administration has been a rewarding and satisfying lifestyle for me for many years.

*Focus makes the most out of every opportunity.*
– UNKNOWN

# HOW EASY IT SEEMED

In 1941, after completing my sophomore year of college, I realized that I would not have the necessary funds to continue college. My solution was to drop out of school and work for a year before returning to college.

I decided to teach school and save enough money to continue my college career. As an eighteen-year-old, I had many obstacles to overcome before securing a teaching position, even in a small country school.

At this time in Texas, a degree was not required, and teaching within a certain field had not come to pass. Colleges offered teaching certificates, but these certificates only indicated that one was qualified to teach and had a certain number of college credits.

I recall being interviewed by a three-person school board for a position in a one-room schoolhouse located deep in the Hill Country of Texas. During the interview, I stated that I lacked three college hours before earning my teaching certification. One board member told me that was all right because I could go down some Saturday morning and get those three hours.

This teaching position sounded promising, but it did not materialize.

*There is no short cut to achievement. Life requires thorough preparation.*
– GEORGE WASHINGTON CARVER

# BAKING ON ONE SIDE WHILE FREEZING ON THE OTHER

My first teaching job was in the Texas Hill Country, which was made up mainly of ranches. The school was twenty-one miles from the nearest town, so I secured a room at a nearby ranch house that had no indoor plumbing and no electricity. Taking a bath was a real challenge. I had to get a number three washtub, place it in front of the fireplace, and build a fire to keep warm. This resulted in a situation whereby I would bake on the side next to the fireplace and freeze on the other side. All this time, the water was losing heat. So, I was taking a cold bath under trying conditions.

Desiring to simplify the bathing process, I discovered a waterfall a mile or so from the ranch house, in an isolated area of the ranch. The flow of the water was adequate, and the bathing area had a rock foundation.

I used this shower all year long. Incidentally, you haven't lived until you've taken a shower under a waterfall in Texas in February!

*Failure is a far better teacher than success.*
– UNKNOWN

# TWENTY-ONE MILES
# DOWN THE RIVER

As I neared the end of my sophomore year in college, I realized I would not have the money to go to college the next year, even though the registration fee for a semester was only twenty-five dollars. You could take as many hours of courses as you thought you could handle, but the cost of room and board plus books would be a problem for me. I decided to work a year and reenter college the next year.

Country schools were scattered throughout the state of Texas. My thought was to teach school for a year, even though I had not taken a single hour of education courses during my first two years of college. I applied at every country school within a twenty-mile radius of my hometown of Killeen, Texas. At that time, the only state requirement to teach was a high school diploma. I found out rather quickly that schools did not have many eighteen-year-old classroom teachers.

I worked during the summer and visited with countless members of many boards of trustees, but to no avail. Time was running out, and I was having no luck. About ten days before school would begin, I heard that there was a vacancy at Spanish Oak School in Burnet County, Texas, about seventy miles from Killeen.

I drove to Burnet, the county seat, to inquire about the location of Spanish Oak School. They referred me to Marble Falls, which was another twenty miles away. I drove to Marble Falls and again inquired about the location of Spanish Oak School. I was advised that it was some twenty-one miles down the river.

Upon arriving in the community of Spanish Oak, I could not find the school. I was able to locate the president of the school board of trustees who confirmed that there was a vacancy. After about fifteen minutes of conversation, he hired me to teach at the Spanish Oak School. He also informed me that classes would start in eight days. When I asked about teacher housing, he told me the teacher usually stayed at the ranch house, which was about two hundred yards from the school.

Incidentally, I had not been able to find the school

because it was located in a small canyon. The road had been washed out, and one had to walk down the hill to get to the school.

I moved into my room at the ranch house on Sunday before school started on Monday. I was excited to see the school and my classroom. After unpacking, I walked over to the school, which was a one-room, unpainted building. There was no electricity, no indoor plumbing, and no lock on the front door. A teacher's desk and twenty student desks were inside, along with a wood-burning stove and a single blackboard.

On Monday, eighteen students showed up for school: one first grader, one second grader, four fourth graders, five sixth graders, four seventh graders, two eighth graders, and one tenth grader. With one teacher and eighteen students scattered over seven grades, one might imagine what the master schedule looked like. However, with the students' help and understanding, it worked out very well.

The students explained to me that the "drinking fountain" was a three-gallon bucket with a single dipper. Water came from a spring some hundred yards from the schoolhouse. I later learned that if I sent girls for the water, they were unable to get close enough to the deep water to avoid having some mud on the rim of the bucket. If I sent boys, they delighted in catching a few tadpoles and placing them in the water so the girls would refuse to drink it.

Class periods were often like a community meeting, with all the students taking part, asking questions and providing answers. Such participation in a one-room schoolhouse meant that a student would likely hear the same lesson a number of times as he or she moved from grade to grade over the period of years.

Like anywhere else, the students here were kids at heart with the same attitudes, problems, and feelings. Gene, an excellent fourth-grade student, could not resist taking part in all of the history lessons. When I asked a US history question and the eighth graders did not answer immediately, he would provide the answer in a loud voice. Later, I noticed when Gene came in from recess, his hair was often uncombed, his clothes would be wrinkled, and patches of dirt were on his pants and shirt. Later, I discovered that when Gene embarrassed Clavin with an unwelcomed answer, Clavin would catch

Gene at recess and try to persuade him to exercise silence during class periods.

All in all, the one year I taught at Spanish Oak was a rewarding and joyful experience that resulted in a number of lifelong friendships.

*In the field of education, success is often an orphan, while failure has many fathers.*
– UNKNOWN

# PAID BY VOUCHER

I was eighteen years old when I began teaching in the early 1940s. I accepted a teaching position in a rural area that was very isolated from the business world. I had not taken any classes in education during my two years of college, and I did not know how or what to teach when I began in that one-room schoolhouse with multiple grade levels.

My monthly salary was $80.00 for teaching, $10.00 for serving as principal, and $7.50 for being the janitor, so my total monthly salary was $97.50. This was not a bad salary for an eighteen-year-old in the 1940s. The teachers in Killeen where I attended high school were only earning eighty dollars per month.

I had to drive twenty-one miles to the county seat to collect my check each month. Once I received the check, I rushed across the street to the only bank in town to cash it. When I presented the check to the bank teller and requested cash, he looked at the check, shook his head, and left the teller station. He returned shortly with the bank president, who explained to me that I had presented the teller with a voucher, not a check. He went on to explain to me that the bank had been accepting vouchers from a number of rural schools, but the state was not redeeming them. He said until the time the state began to pay off the vouchers, the bank was not accepting any more. He returned the voucher to me.

After giving the situation some thought, I decided to drive the seventy-two miles to my hometown of Killeen to talk to my uncle, who was president of the bank there.

My uncle examined the voucher and told me that they had accepted the vouchers in the past but were not accepting them now. However, in my case, he would accept my voucher, adding a 15 percent charge. This meant the bank would take $14.63 of my earnings to cash the voucher.

I did this every month during the school year. Oh, well, it was a lesson learned.

*Not knowing what you don't know can be an expensive venture.*
– UNKNOWN

# A BARBER BY APPOINTMENT

THREE WEEKS AFTER STARTING MY TEACHING POSITION in Spanish Oak School in Burnett County, Texas, I was surprised on a Saturday morning when a lady drove up to the ranch house where I lived. She had three school-age boys riding in the back of her pickup. Her statement to me was, "The last teacher we had here cut the students' hair every Saturday morning. I hope you are prepared to do the same." She left all three boys and took off to parts unknown.

I was not going to admit that a former teacher could do something I couldn't do, so I set up a makeshift barber's chair and began to cut the boys' hair. I was determined to prove my talent as a barber.

I did what you might call a terrace cut. I called it that because one could see the scalp after each of my cuts into the abundance of hair on each boy. Soon the mother returned to pick up her sons. When she saw their haircut style, she sighed, took a deep breath, and said a weak *thank you* and departed.

The haircut I gave the boys must have been outstanding and long lasting because the lady never returned with her sons for another haircut. The word must have spread in the community – no one ever again approached me for any more barber work.

*There are many paths to the top of the mountain, but only one view.*
– HARRY MILLNER

# ELSIE

I often wonder what happened to Elsie. During my first year of teaching, Elsie was in the first grade.

With only two years of college and not a single college hour of what or how to teach, I was employed as a teacher at a one-room school in Burnet County, Texas, called Spanish Oak School. I was the only applicant for the job and was lucky to be employed.

Eighteen students reported to class on the first day of school. Elsie was the only first grader, along with one second grader, four fourth graders, five sixth graders, four seventh graders, two eighth graders, and one tenth grader.

Because this was a one-room school building with only the one classroom, I taught all the students at the same time. Looking back, I realize that by the end of that school year, Elsie was probably the champion student of coloring between the lines in the entire county. I had little or no idea of what a first grader should learn, except to color. My solution was to have her sit next to an eighth-grade girl who was to help her with assignments and directions.

As the school year went along, I learned more of what a first grader was expected to learn; however, my instruction was inadequate. It has now been seventy-three years since Elsie was in first grade, and I am still haunted because of the job I did *not* do as Elsie's first-grade teacher.

I still wonder what happened to Elsie.

*The leader's objective is to leverage the strengths of people and make their weaknesses become irrelevant.*
– PETER PRUCKER

# SHOOT THE PRINCIPAL

During the mid-1950s, Killeen schools added a visiting teacher to its staff, a position funded by the state. The title of the position had many interpretations; however, the one used by Killeen was truant officer or "Hooky Cop," as the students named the position. In reality, the visiting teacher was to make house calls to any home where the student had been absent for any unexplained reason.

In some cases, legal encouragement was used in the event the family was hesitant to cooperate with the state-required attendance policy. This position was new to the Killeen community, so there were times when individual family members resented the visits. They sometimes interpreted the policy as an infringement on their independence.

Such was the case when I, as principal, asked the visiting teacher to call on a family with three school-aged children who had just moved into the community. Their residence was only three blocks from the Avenue

D Elementary School campus. It was quite evident when their kids were not in school. The visiting teacher did make the house call and explained the state attendance law to the mother, who took exception to the visit and inquired as to who was responsible for requiring the visit.

The visiting teacher explained the attendance law and stated that legal action could be taken if the children were not in school on a regular basis. To this the mother replied, "Who did you say ordered the visit?"

The visiting teacher replied, "It was the principal of Avenue D Elementary School. In fact, you can see his office from here." He then pointed to the three-story red-brick building on the hill. He further stated, "His office is on the second floor."

The mother replied, "I will send my kids to school when I think it is necessary, and tell that principal that I plan to shoot him!"

The visiting teacher could not wait to get back to school and advise me that my life had been threatened.

We did not take the threat as a serious concern; however, it often crossed my mind as I moved about the office, which had three rows of windows across the side of the building that faced her house. The next day, the visiting teacher walked into my office with a sign pinned on his coat that said, "I am not the principal." He was followed by the assistant principal, who wore a sign that said, "I am not the principal either." Then came the janitor with a sign that read, "I am only the janitor."

Several uneventful days went by. I smoked a pipe in those days, and administrators were allowed to smoke in their offices. One of the above-mentioned group had placed small explosive loads in my tobacco pouch. A salesman called on me that day, and as we stood in front of "the" window, I placed tobacco in my pipe and lit it, only to have at least three of the loads go off. Since I had recently been discharged from the army and with thoughts of the mother down the street, I hit the floor for protection. Much laughter could be heard from down the hall.

I do not know what the salesman was selling because he never came back!

*The future ain't what it used to be.*
– YOGI BERRA

# THE GRADE BOOK

After finishing college and spending four years in the army, I returned to my hometown to assume the position of principal of the only elementary school in Killeen, Texas. The school building, when I attended classes there, was a three-story red-brick building.

Because of World War II and the location of Fort Hood, the town had grown, and school enrollment had also increased. With the increased enrollment, the red-brick building had become the site for only the elementary grades. I occupied what had been the superintendent's office which had an old slide-top desk in it. Since only elementary-age students were enrolled in the school, it was difficult for me to see the students who came into the office because of the height of the desk.

Therefore, I asked the custodian to remove the roll-top portion of the desk. When he returned it to me, he stated that he had found a number of articles down behind the roll top. One of the items he recovered was an old 1932 student grade book. As I thumbed through the grade book, I found my name recorded as a fifth grader. Also, beside my name was this statement: "Talks too much." Also recorded in red pencil beside another classmate's name was the word "Slow." That person was now the town's mayor.

The grade book belonged to Miss Wiggom, who had been a teacher at the elementary school in 1932. In due time, she married and stopped teaching to raise her family. Several years later, she returned to teaching. As fate would have it, she was one of the teachers in the school where I was serving as principal. This was too much of an opportunity for fun to let it go by, so I called her on the phone and told her I had found a mistake in one of her past grade books. I asked her to come by the office at her convenience to discuss the matter. She expressed genuine concern and apologized for such a mistake.

That afternoon, I heard her high-heel shoes coming toward my office. Upon entering the office, she asked to see the mistake. I produced the grade book that was faded, wrinkled, and timeworn. She looked at it and turned it over as I referred to the page with the "mistakes."

When she recognized the grade book, she noted the year and the other details, and she said, "No, that is not a mistake, and it still stands today!"

*Leadership does not depend on being right.*
– IVAN ILLICH

# TRIGGER GORMLEY

WHILE SERVING AS PRINCIPAL OF AVENUE D ELEMENTARY School in Killeen, Texas, in the 1950s, I admired the students who attended school every day, rain or shine. The school system was growing so rapidly that classrooms were made in some of the old army barracks which had been relocated near the main building of the school.

I always admired Trigger Gormley because of his perfect attendance. He never missed a day. When I made my supervisory rounds, either in the morning or in the afternoon, I always found him lying in the entryway to the fourth-grade barracks. You see, Trigger Gormley was a collie dog. His owner was a fourth-grade student named Butch Gormley. Trigger was waiting for Butch to be released from school so they could walk home together. Trigger was an accepted feature of the school population, and he never bothered anyone and made friends easily.

I accepted Trigger as a symbol of the student body. At

the end of the year, when promotions were presented to the student body, I presented Trigger Gormley a certificate of attendance for being neither absent nor tardy for the entire school year.

*Rise from the bottom, soar to the top. Your ambitions are endless. You'll never stop.*
– JAMES FLETSHER, HIGH SCHOOL STUDENT, RMA

# IDENTICAL TWINS

WHEN TEACHING SCHOOL, I HAD MY FIRST EXPERIENCE in dealing with identical twins in my classroom. The twins were Wilford and Winford, and they were identical in every respect. In time, my solution to identify each one was to paint the lobe of the right ear of one of the boys with mercurochrome. This solution only worked for one day, as the next day both boys had painted the lobes of their right ears.

At another time, while I was teaching senior English, it was a requirement that book reports be given orally during a teacher-student conference. The identical twins this year were Harold and Howell. The rumors around campus were that these two young men took great delight in impersonating each other. The prior school year, they had done this during the teacher-student conference when presenting the book report. It had taken some time, but I gradually became more prepared to deal with such situations. Both young men had book reports scheduled on the same day. My plan was to place a small amount of chalk dust on the back of the chair on which each student would sit. In came Harold, who went through the book report routine. Then, sure enough, next came "Howell" to report on the same book. However, "Howell" had a telltale amount of chalk dust on his back. So, my plan worked – Harold was prepared to give the report over again. There was no credit for book reports on this day for either Harold or Howell.

*Pair up in threes.*
– YOGI BERRA

# THE OTHER SIDE OF THE HILL

After returning from the army in 1946, I secured a job as an assistant football coach for the junior varsity football team which had a separate schedule from the varsity and usually played on Thursday nights.

During the war, no cars or buses were made for public sale. My school district was hard-pressed to keep their fleet of school buses in operating condition. The junior varsity team was provided an old bus for their scheduled out-of-town games. The motor in the bus would start and run without any trouble, but it did not have enough power to climb a hill.

Going up a hill with a forty-five-degree incline normally required the team to get out and push the bus as it neared the top to get it over the hill. Then the team would run to catch the bus as it descended the other side of the hill. This action was required several times going and coming from the games.

Several times, the head coach came to the game to

critique our performance. He frequently told me that the team seemed tired and lacked enthusiasm for the game. Since he did not ride the bus with us to out-of-town games, I was never able to convince him that the team was tired and unenthusiastic from pushing the bus up and over the hills and then chasing the bus to get back on board.

I only stayed in that coaching position for a few years. Unfortunately for the team, they still had the same bus when I left.

*If you come to a fork in the road, take it.*
– YOGI BERRA

# HOW DO I SMELL FROM HERE?

IMMEDIATELY AFTER MY DISCHARGE FROM THE ARMY at the end of World War II, I was employed as a school principal and coach in the Killeen School System. At that time, coaches and players stood along the sidelines of the field to allow for more contact with game officials.

During a game with Belton High School, the officials made several calls against the Killeen team. As the game progressed, it seemed to me that the officials were going out of their way to find ways to penalize our team. I yelled at the officials from time to time, expressing my feelings toward their officiating.

On one occasion, the official called roughing the passer, a fifteen-yard penalty against Killeen, to which I yelled to the official, "You stink!" The official picked up the ball and marched off fifteen additional yards.

He placed the ball on the ground, turned to look at me, and said, "How do I smell from here?"

I did not reply.

*Common sense does not grow in every garden.*
– UNKNOWN

# UNCONTROLLED SPENDING

I SUPPOSE OUTFITTING A JUNIOR HIGH FOOTBALL TEAM has seldom been a priority with a superintendent or business manager in a small school system. To illustrate, I was the principal and football coach in Killeen, Texas, in the 1950s.

One summer, I noted that the jerseys of the football uniforms were worn and somewhat ragged. So, I approached the superintendent to ask if we could purchase new jerseys. He asked me how many I would need. I told him we could do with twenty-two. Next, he asked how much they would cost. I told him $1.76 each. To my surprise, he raised his voice as he informed me that we must stop this uncontrolled spending in this school district! We must stop buying what we don't need.

With this answer, I assumed my request had been denied.

The team banded together and sold boxes of greeting cards to raise the necessary funds. The team proudly took to the field in September with new $1.76 jerseys.

*Together we can achieve more.*
– UNKNOWN

# MOTIVATION AT ITS LOWEST

AFTER LEAVING THE MILITARY SERVICE AT THE END OF World War II, I took a job coaching the junior varsity football team in Killeen. I had been coaching for several years when we were playing Cameron, Texas. It was halftime, and the score was nine to seven in favor of Cameron. My motivational speech at the halftime break included a personal reference.

I informed the team that we had worked hard together all year and for some members of our squad a period of two years. I had taught them all I knew about football, and I wanted them to go back on the field and be determined to use all they had learned from my coaching and defeat Cameron.

Well, things didn't work out like I had envisioned. The game ended with a score of thirty-three to seven, Cameron's favor. It was at this time when I began to wonder if coaching was my calling. After a few weeks, I decided to go into school administration, where I remained for the next forty-four years.

*There is no worse mistake in public leadership than to hold out false hopes soon to be swept away.*
– WINSTON CHURCHILL

# SAM REID—A LASTING IMPRESSION

I CAN CLOSE MY EYES AND SEE HIM TODAY. SAM WAS A student in Killeen Junior High School during the early 1950s. I first came in contact with Sam when I coached junior varsity football. He was likeable, friendly, polite, and he displayed a positive attitude. He captured the people's hearts because he was always smiling.

I was also Sam's principal, and I taught him in my language arts class. I could see myself in Sam in many of his study habits. Sam always seemed to make failing grades on his spelling tests. In my flawed judgment, I had convinced myself that the reason Sam failed the weekly tests was because he did not study. I wanted Sam to be successful. One time, I became so exasperated that I took him into the bookroom and administered corporal punishment. I was hoping to instill in him the fact that he needed to study for the spelling tests.

Sam was almost six feet tall and weighed about 160 pounds. After I completed his punishment, he turned to me, put his arms around me, and said, "Mr. Hall, I still love you." That statement hurt me to the quick. After what I had done to him, he could still make such a statement!

Sam's statement gave me a new awakening in analyzing students' problems. I began searching for reasons and answers rather than making snap judgments. I later found out that Sam was dyslexic. He did not see letters and words like most students did. I continued to work with him all through high school. I did not improve his spelling, but he caused me to become a better teacher and a more understanding person.

He went on to become a fine football player in high school. After graduation, he enlisted in the army and planned to make his career in the military. For a few years, Sam would visit my family and me when he was back in Killeen. After a period of time, our paths didn't cross as frequently. Sam was relocated for another military placement, but he continued to serve in the army.

A few years later, I heard Sam had passed away while in military service. I never did find out the circumstances of his death, but I know one thing: I loved Sam Reid!

*Value each relationship—treat each person with respect.*
– STEVE KRUSICH

# THE MAGIC BASKETBALL COURT

WHEN I WAS DISCHARGED FROM THE ARMY IN 1946, I was selected as principal of Killeen Public School. I learned almost immediately that being a principal meant you were also coach of the football team and baseball teams.

As the year progressed, the boys began to request a basketball team be formed. I explained that we did not have a gym, so all the games would be played away. Furthermore, we did not even have an outdoor court on which to practice. We did have two outdoor blacktop tennis courts. In time, basketball goals were installed at each end of the courts. There were no sidelines or boundaries marked, but free-throw circles were marked off.

Students showed a surprising amount of enthusiasm for the game. The rules of the game were explained and enforced. We began to schedule games at nearby school districts. The team had won nearly half of their games, as well as two tournaments during that first year.

The season of the second year came along, and I was again surprised at the ability and determination of the team. As the season progressed, the team began to win almost all of their games. Opposing coaches expressed amazement at our winning record because they knew we had no gym in which to practice.

Please remember, I finished high school in Killeen in 1939. There was no gym and no basketball team at that time. I had never played basketball and had seen very few games. I noticed that our team seemed to be in better physical condition than the other teams we played which led to our team scoring more points toward the end of the game.

Later in the year, we were playing a team in the Belton School District when one of the coaches told me that they intended to build a new gym with two regulation basketball courts. His statement about a regulation court stuck in my mind. Remember, I had never played basketball and did not know the dimensions of a regulation court. I found the dimensions to be eighty-four feet long. When I measured our practice court, it was 120 feet long.

Need I say more?

*Finding a player is easy. Getting them to play as a team is another story.*
– CASEY STENGEL

# SEARCHING FOR THE SECOND-DUMBEST ONE IN THE CLASS

IN THE 1950S WHEN I SERVED AS SECONDARY PRINCIPAL in the Killeen school system, Mary Hornbuckle was a faculty member who taught English. To say she was from the "old school" would be a gross understatement. She was an excellent teacher who took very few excuses for nonperformance by students.

Her classes were strictly subject-matter centered, with little curricular activities. Her teaching style required strict attention from the students, with no exceptions. She often put down students who gave the wrong answer. For example, she once asked a student to define a noun. The student replied, "It is the name of anything." Miss Hornbuckle said, "That is wrong. What does the second-dumbest one in the class think it might be?"

Miss Hornbuckle and I worked together for almost nine years. I spent a great deal of my time with parents defending her teaching style. Students seldom complained. They seemed to take pride in the fact that they "survived" a year of Miss Hornbuckle's class.

On two occasions, Jim Gold failed to turn in his homework assignments. Miss Hornbuckle chewed him up one side and down the other. Then she told him to report to her room after school was out. She told him, "I am going to teach you some English and how to do your homework."

Later in the year, Jim's mother requested that he be transferred out of Miss Hornbuckle's class, and I approved the transfer. When I told Jim that his mother had requested a transfer to another teacher's English class, he said, "No, please leave me in Miss Hornbuckle's class. She is the only teacher who seems to care whether I learn or not." So, Jim remained in her class.

During the remainder of the year, it was not unusual to see Jim meet Miss Hornbuckle in the parking lot, helping her bring her books and other items into her room. I always thought she had tough love for her students, and they knew it.

As time moved on, I was pleasantly surprised to see

Miss Hornbuckle's former students return from college to visit her. They always thanked her for preparing them for college work.

*Leadership is the lifting of a person's vision to high sights.*
– PETER DRUCKER

# DIDN'T I MENTION
# THAT TO YOU?

IN 1947, I WAS THE "B" TEAM FOOTBALL COACH IN Killeen. We usually played eleven-man football, but Copperas Cove, a small community near Killeen, played six-man football. The Copperas Cove team was outstanding. When the season ended, someone suggested that my "B" team in Killeen play the Copperas Cove "A" team in a six-man football game.

I contacted Coach J. L. Williams, the Copperas Cove coach, to ask if he would be interested in playing a six-man football game against my "B" team. In a few days, the proper approvals were given, and the game was scheduled with the chamber of commerce's sponsorship.

I was not completely clear on the rules for six-man football, so Coach Williams met with me several times to discuss the difference in the rules when playing six-man football in comparison to eleven-man football. Coach

Williams was very patient with me because I had so many questions.

I put my team through the paces. The team was taught the new rules as we continued to prepare for the game.

Finally, game day arrived, and a sizable crowd was present to watch. Copperas Cove won the toss, so we kicked off to them. They returned the ball to the thirty-yard line. On the first play of the game, they passed the ball to the center, who ran for a touchdown.

I immediately ran out on the field to talk to the referee. I explained to him that the center caught the ball and ran for the touchdown. The referee informed me that this is legal in six-man football. By this time, Coach Williams had joined us on the field. I turned to him and said, "The referee says it is legal for the center to catch a forward pass."

Coach Williams said, "Yes, that's right."

I said, "Coach, you never mentioned that."

Coach Williams replied, "Didn't I mention that to you?"

That was the first of many rules I learned about six-man football for the first time that night.

*Success is not an accident. It is preceded by*
*anticipation, planning, and preparing.*
– THE NATIONAL ASSOCIATION OF
SCHOOL SUPERINTENDENTS

# A GREAT SMALL TOWN

After serving as a public-school principal for sixteen years, I was elected superintendent of the Lampasas Public Schools. Lampasas is the county seat of Lampasas County and is located on the edge of the famous Hill Country in Texas. The population at that time was 5,611, and the school enrollment was approaching 1,800.

Lampasas was a friendly small town where the people all knew each other, and I enjoyed a great relationship with many of the citizens.

During my third year as superintendent, I gained the friendship of a young officer of one of the local banks. We were not close friends, but our professions caused us to have business dealings. We learned to respect each other.

During the early part of my fourth year in Lampasas, the public learned my banker friend had been diagnosed with advanced stages of leukemia. He had time to plan his own funeral, and I was selected to be one of his pallbearers. His wife later told me I had been selected as a "new friend." I still remember the look on the faces of some of the attendees at the funeral as I joined the other pallbearers during the funeral. They were very surprised at such a "newcomer" to the community being selected for such an honor.

To me, Lampasas was an all-American hometown, a great place to raise a family. We lived there eight wonderful years. I have to admit, it was the best job I ever had; however, I became ambitious and wanted to be superintendent at a larger school. Upon finding a new position, we left Lampasas but never forgot the good times and good people there.

*Where do you spend most of your time in your mind?*
- *Imagination*
- *Present*
- *Past*
- *Future*
– UNKNOWN

# TWO BLANKETS UNDER THE BRIDGE

It was like she said: there were two blankets hanging down from under the bridge. We surmised they were hanging there to provide a modest amount of privacy. This was where the girl and her father lived. The girl was around fourteen or fifteen years of age.

A resident in the area had observed the girl from time to time as she came and went to the bridge location. The resident had advised the school nurse of the girl's situation. The school leaders were interested in inviting her to attend school. Realizing that this could be a ticklish undertaking, the nurse asked me to go along and attempt to make contact with the girl at the bridge.

We parked on a side street that had access to the area underneath the bridge. We saw the two blankets hanging from underneath, but no girl. We observed six or so other areas where people evidently slept at times. We found the girl washing clothes on the riverbank. We introduced ourselves and informed the girl that our purpose for the visit was to invite her to attend school. She introduced herself as Marylou. She was very polite and well-mannered. She asked a number of questions regarding the location of the school and other related information.

Marylou agreed to come to school but commented that she had no money and that her clothes were not very nice. The nurse agreed to pick her up the next morning at seven forty-five near the road where we had parked. Marylou seemed eager to take part in school activities. She especially enjoyed the school lunch period. She made friends easily and enjoyed the library and the reading materials that were available.

Marylou and the school nurse became close in their friendship. Marylou brought extra clothes to school from time to time. This gave the school nurse the opportunity to take the clothes to the athletic department where she washed, dried, and even pressed whatever Marylou brought.

For the next three weeks, it was a pleasure to see Marylou blend in with the school setting. However, after a time, Marylou did not come to school each day.

The nurse and I returned to the bridge to inquire as to her whereabouts. This time, the father was there. When we asked about Marylou, he was unfriendly and very defensive. He said we had caused her to be unsatisfied with the life he had provided her. He told us we were not welcome to have anything more to do with her. At this point, Marylou spoke up and said, "But, Dad, I like the school and the people there." At this point, the father hit her across the face with his open hand and told her to follow him.

Three days later, the neighbor called and stated that it seemed that Marylou and her father were preparing to move from the bridge. The nurse insisted that we go to the bridge and observe what was taking place. As we passed the railroad yard that was located on the other side of the bridge, we saw Marylou and her father beside the train. The father pitched a bundle into a boxcar. He then jumped onto the train through the open door, extended his hand, and helped Marylou board the train.

As I glanced at the nurse, tears were rolling down her cheeks. I kept my emotions to myself but realized we had lost another battle in trying to help another student find a way toward a new life.

Guilt was written all over the ceiling as I lay awake that night, staring into space far past midnight. What had we done wrong? What could we have done differently to gain the father's confidence and understanding? How many other Marylou's are lost to a decent future?

*We must not, we just cannot afford the great waste*
*that comes from the neglect of a single child.*
– LYNDON B. JOHNSON

# THE LAMPASAS RESEARCH STUDY

During the early 1960s, the Lampasas School System was one of nineteen school districts selected by the United States Department of Education to participate in an eight-year study. The purpose of the study was to determine what the earliest predictor might be of success as a graduate.

The study selected all students in fifth grade and was designed to track the individual student from grade five through grade twelve, with a focus on each student's progress toward graduation. Many observations and evaluations were built into the study.

I became the superintendent in Lampasas during the fourth year of the eight-year study. The study was designed to gather information considered personal concerning the family of each participant.

Of the nineteen schools selected for the study, eighteen of them completed the project. The information gathered from the study was submitted to a team of researchers at the US Department of Education.

After a while, the results of the study were released to the public. The researchers determined that how a student ranked in fifth grade was the best predictor of success seven years later.

*Alone we can do so little—together we can do so much.*
– UNKNOWN

# PAPER TOWELS AND YEARS GONE BY

My first position as superintendent of schools was in Lampasas, Texas. Our older son, Skip, was in college, and our younger son, Charlie, was in fifth grade.

Charlie was an active, talkative student who enjoyed school and all the activities that went along with it. Charlie's teacher was Mrs. Cole, a lovely lady with a sense of humor who was an excellent teacher.

I am sure Charlie's constant talking without permission had begun to irritate Mrs. Cole. On one occasion, shortly after Thanksgiving, she took paper towels, wadded them up, and placed them in Charlie's mouth. Then she placed a loose-fitting piece of tape over his mouth.

Mrs. Cole called me that night to explain what had happened. I told her, "You don't worry about it. You did exactly right." The kids made Charlie feel like a hero. Mrs. Cole became one of Charlie's favorite teachers.

The school had to order more paper towels during

that year. I am sure the reason was that teachers thought if you could stuff paper towels in the mouth of the superintendent's child, you could also do it to some of the other free talkers.

*Laughter is sunshine in the schoolhouse.*
– MARK LUKERT

# A HOLE IN A SHOE

During the early 1960s, I became superintendent of the Lampasas School System. Lampasas is a nice town in the beginning of the Hill Country, and it has always been a choice place to live and raise a family in Texas.

During this time, I became active in the Methodist church. I served as a steward, lay leader, and Sunday-school teacher. During one of our services, church members were invited to go forward to the area of the church known as the prayer rail, where the members would kneel in prayer. My wife, Billye, and I did as requested.

The next Monday, I left the office for lunch. When I returned, there was a gift-wrapped package on my desk. Upon opening the package, I found a new pair of shoes with a note saying some people didn't know when they needed a new pair of shoes.

As it turned out, when I had knelt at the prayer rail, the bottoms of my shoes were exposed revealing a hole in one shoe. The president of the school board was also a member of the congregation, hence the attention to my shoe. The fun part of the incident was that in a joking manner, members of the congregation asked the board president if they could not afford a pay raise for the superintendent. The answer was, "The hole is not that big."

*Don't worry about the horse being blind. Just load the wagon.*
– JOHN MADDEN

# A WARNING TOO LATE

During the late 1960s when I was serving as superintendent of the Lampasas Public Schools, football was an important part of community life. Even the perceived success of the school administration and especially the superintendent was measured by the win-loss record of the football team. It was also very important that the superintendent was seen at each of the ten scheduled games.

Upon one occasion, our team was scheduled to play a game in Mason, about eighty miles away, and I was late leaving Lampasas. I was attempting to make up time by speeding down highway 281, which is usually not crowded. My wife and our younger son were with me.

Charlie had developed an interest in the speed limit on any given section of the highway. He was small enough that he could stand on the floorboard of the back seat and look over my shoulder where he could see the speedometer. At first, he told me I was speeding. But as I grew tired of his reminders, I reprimanded him and advised him that I did not need someone quoting the speed limit to me. So he proceeded to ask his mother what the speed limit was, even though he knew exactly what it was.

On this occasion, I was driving well over the posted speed limit at almost eighty miles an hour. As we topped a hill, we met a highway patrolman going the opposite way. Charlie took it upon himself to inform me of the actions of the officer. "Daddy, he is turning around. Daddy, he has turned on his roof lights. Daddy, he is coming up fast. Daddy, he wants you to stop."

Well, I stopped. The patrolman came to my side of the car. He asked, as they usually do, "Sir, is there some kind of emergency?" I told him I was on my way to a high school football game. He asked if I was connected with the school system, and I explained I was the superintendent.

After some dialogue concerning Lampasas and football, the officer said, "Mr. Hall, I understand your desire to get to the game, but the very least I can do is give you a warning ticket."

Suddenly, from the back seat, with his face between the patrolman and my face, Charlie said, "Dad, I've been warning you!" I never knew what happened to the warning ticket. I know I did not get it. My ticket was of the pay-the-fine kind.

I assumed the patrolman surmised that Charlie had been warning me about speeding and I had paid no attention. So the patrolman thought he would add emphasis to Charlie's "safety program."

*You cannot increase achievement without some form of accountability.*
– ROD PAGE

# THE ANDREWS SCHOOL BOARD

My first service as a school superintendent was in Lampasas, Texas. In educational circles, Lampasas was referred to as a poor district because of the low assessment values assigned to ranch- and farmland. Living and working in Lampasas was a pleasant experience. My family and I have many fond memories of our eight years there, and it may have been the best job I ever had.

I became ambitious while living in Lampasas and wanted a larger challenge. In the 1970s, I assumed the superintendent position in the Andrews Independent School District. Andrews was a country district consisting of some fifteen hundred square miles in the center of the west Texas oilfields, with eleven thousand producing oil wells. Andrews ISD was one of the richest school districts in Texas. It was the first school district to have all schools air conditioned. The high school was the first to have carpet throughout the building. The school had purchased Greyhound buses to transport their athletic teams to out-of-town events. And at that time, their teachers were the highest paid in the state.

This is the situation I inherited when I moved to Andrews. It was completely different than the "poor" district I had left in Lampasas.

Since I had never been to a national school board convention, I was excited when the board president informed me that all the Andrews board, the school attorney, the superintendent, and all the wives always attended the conference. There would be a total of eighteen people. I was asked to make the necessary arrangements, which I was happy to do.

A few weeks later, the board president called to ask if I had made the arrangements. I responded affirmatively. He asked what arrangements I had made with the airline. I proudly replied, "Why, coach, of course."

He said, "I was afraid you might do that. We fly first class. Please revise the reservations."

The convention was in San Francisco, California. Once we arrived, we attended the convention during the day and went sightseeing at night. The board president informed me that one of the board members had been stationed near Carmel while serving in the navy. It had been decided that the group would spend one day in and around Carmel. He asked me to arrange for the rented cars. On the day of the trip, we went to pick up the cars (economy class—Fords). When we arrived back at the hotel with the three cars, the board vice president came out and said, "What are you doing with this type of car?"

I said, "They did not have the compact cars."

He said, "Okay, get out. I will go make the arrangements."

So help me! In about thirty minutes, he arrived with three black Lincoln Town Cars with chauffeurs. Thus, we made our trip to Carmel.

I told my wife I was not sure I could become accustomed to this type of arrangements. Her reply was, "Please try."

*We get better results when we take calculated risks.*
– CHRIS SKIPPER

# THE SCHOOL BOARD
# POLICY HANDBOOK

During the 1960s, school administrators and school board members began to pay a great deal of attention to policies and the legal aspects related to the operation of the public schools.

Many schools did not even have stated policies, much less have them in an organized form. While serving as superintendent of schools in Andrews, Texas, I became interested in school policies and how we might present them to the staff, parents, and public. In many situations, board involvement with written policies meant receiving a single sheet of paper with a copy of one policy being discussed at a time.

Our solution to the problem was to employ an individual in Austin, Texas, with a legal background to write and organize a school policy manual. This he did for the sum of $1,500.

The manual served us well. We shared it with

neighboring school districts and received some acknowledgment for the organization of the manual. The next year, we received a call from an individual who said he had signed a contract with the Texas State Board Association to prepare a manual to be endorsed by the association and distributed to local districts on a for-sale basis. He also stated that he had a copy of our policy manual and asked if he could use a large part of it in his publication. He asked if he could use the Andrews Policy Manual without reference to Andrews. The reason for this request was that because the Andrews school system had all this wealth, other districts might be less inclined to follow it. We agreed. The policy manual was developed for the school board association and widely distributed throughout the state.

We hid our pride and self-satisfaction.

*You can accomplish anything in life, provided that you do not mind who gets the credit.*
– HARRY S. TRUMAN

# THE QUESTION

IT WAS GREAT TO BE THE SUPERINTENDENT OF THE Andrews school system, a single-school district in a county of fifteen hundred square miles with eleven thousand producing oil wells that were served by twenty-two oil and natural-gas companies.

When I was selected for the position, I was told by neighboring superintendents that the position would be good for me monetarily but not good for me professionally. Sure enough, a few years later, I grew ambitious and wanted to move to an even larger school system. When I was being interviewed by the school board of a larger school district, this question was always asked: how much does your current district spend per child per year?

When I answered $11,300, which was sometimes twice the amount that many of the other school districts could afford, my interview was all but over.

*Those who look for the bad in people will surely find it.*
– ABRAHAM LINCOLN

# AN EXTRA YEAR OF DEVELOPMENT

IN THE EARLY 1980S, IT BECAME COMMON KNOWLEDGE that a number of parents were holding male students back from being promoted to the next grade level in order for the boys to receive an extra year of physical development before entering high school.

This was taking place at a number of schools all over the country. I was serving as superintendent of a school during this time and observed this firsthand. Administrators normally discouraged this practice; however, some football coaches encouraged it.

The television show *60 Minutes* heard of the practice and presented a section on one of its programs where they exposed it. At the school where I was, a *60 Minutes* truck pulled into the junior high school football field on a Thursday afternoon. The reporters asked permission to enter the end zone of the playing field. They had already made arrangements with the opposing team for the filming of their athletics.

I lost some respect for the integrity of the program when I observed the events that took place during this game. Near the end of the playing time, a player from the opposing team was hurt. The coach went onto the field and appeared to be administrating first aid to the injured player. After a few minutes, the coach picked him up in his arms and began carrying him off the field. One of the boy's arms was dangling and flopping back and forth as the coach proceeded to the sideline. We later learned that this action had been arranged by the narrator of this section of the program. Even in junior high games, if a player is injured and needs to be removed from the field, a stretcher is used, and the arms would not be dangling as he is moved from the field.

When the program was broadcast several weeks later, it was implied that parents were holding back the male students for another year to provide additional physical development.

*It's the soldier, not the reporter, who has*
*given us the freedom of the press.*
– UNKNOWN

# FOOTBALL—RODEOING— WELDING

When I was superintendent of a west Texas school district in the heart of the oil-producing area, money was plentiful. Football was the top sport for most of the west Texas communities, but we often had difficulty finding top-notch players. We did have one young player who stood out as a sophomore when he was playing on the junior varsity team. His friends called him Bugor.

Bugor continued to develop physically and athletically. When he was a junior in high school, he began to blossom as a gifted quarterback. His leadership along with his running and passing ability set him apart from most of the other players in the area. The head coach was very interested in what Bugor did during the summer. He wanted to make sure he was healthy for the next football season.

Early in June, the coach was horrified when he learned that Bugor was riding bulls on the rodeo circuit in west

Texas and even at the Fort Worth rodeo. The coach discussed the dangers of rodeoing with the young man. He told him that any injury could cause him to be unable to play football during the coming football season. He stressed the fact that such an injury might cause him to lose the possibility of a college scholarship.

Bugor seemed to understand and agreed to forgo the rodeo circuit during the current rodeo season. As the summer continued, Bugor's absences at different social events began to be noticeable and of concern to the coach. Upon further investigation, it became apparent that Bugor had gone to work in a nearby oilfield. As more details of Bugor's employment surfaced, the coach wanted to see firsthand the kind of job Bugor was doing. He found that Bugor was working for an oilfield service company about twenty miles out of town.

The coach was determined to find out exactly what kind of job Bugor was doing and went to a part of the oilfield where pipeline was being installed. When he approached the area, he was stopped by a guard and informed that due to the dangers involved in laying pipeline, all nonemployees of the oil company were restricted from the immediate area. When more details came to light, it was revealed that Bugor was working in an extremely dangerous profession. The coach explained to Bugor that welding in the oilfield was more dangerous than riding in the rodeo circuit.

As it turned out, Burgor left the oilfield and returned to high school. He played football during his senior year, and, sure enough, he received a football scholarship to the University of Texas.

*America is too great for small dreams.*
– RONALD REAGAN

# NO DRIVER'S LICENSE NEEDED

DURING THE 1970S, I SERVED AS SUPERINTENDENT OF the Andrews Independent School District. School buses served the rural areas that were on paved or gravel roads. One Saturday morning, a rancher called me and asked if I would meet him at a local coffee shop. When we met, he explained to me the situation he faced. He lived in a remote area of the school district only two miles from the New Mexico state line. He lived less than three miles from the community of Jal, New Mexico. Because of the remote location, the Andrews School District paid the tuition for his three children to attend the Jal schools. His wife taught in Jal, so transportation was not a problem.

Tests had recently revealed that his son, who would be in the fifth grade the next school year, was in need of speech therapy, a service the Jal schools did not offer. Andrews schools provided this therapy for their students. The rancher was questioning how close the Andrews school buses came to his home. We determined that the bus came to the end of a gravel road that was eight miles from his home. After I revealed this information, the rancher stated that his son would meet the bus each day at the end of the gravel road.

I explained to the rancher that much of his time would be spent traveling to and from the bus stop area. The rancher's reply was, "Oh, I won't take him to the bus. We have an old car he can drive to and from home to meet the bus."

My reaction to this response was, "Due to his age, he cannot secure a driver's license."

The rancher answered, "Mister, he will be on my ranch all the way! He will not need a driver's license."

As it turned out, the rancher had a plan for modifying the car so the boy could drive it. He welded extensions on the clutch and brake of the old car. He stacked two wooden Coke boxes that were covered with a quilt on the seat so the boy could see out while guiding the car.

Our bus driver reported that it was quite a show to watch as the boy came over the hill. The boy's limited driving skills and his love of speed were obvious to our bus driver.

I was in the district for two additional years after the boy began meeting the bus. During those two years, he continued to drive to the bus on time and safely.

*Great leaders are almost always great simplifiers,*
*who can cut through argument, debate, and doubt*
*to offer a solution everybody can understand.*
– GENERAL COLIN POWELL

# SEVENTEEN TOUCHES

When I was forty-seven years of age and superintendent of schools in Andrews, Texas, I began to reflect on my own days as a student in high school. I reasoned that during my four years of high school, one teacher had had a profound influence on my life.

I composed a letter to him in which I thanked him for his influence. I noted that even after all this time (twenty-nine years), I still recall seventeen times when he had either touched me or said something to me that made my day. Small things provided encouragement and stimulated my ambition.

His everyday actions made me feel that he cared about me as a student and was willing to demonstrate such feelings. I was assigned a front seat in study hall, a room that was perhaps three times as large as a regular classroom. Many times, when he came to the study hall to make announcements, he stood by my desk as he made the announcement. He did not look at me, but he would place his hand on my shoulder. He made the announcement and walked away. I always felt ten feet tall!

Woodrow Young never responded to my letter; however, after his funeral some fifteen years later, his wife told me that my letter was among his possessions in his safe-deposit box. I was forever glad I wrote the letter.

*There are always flowers for those who want to see them.*
– HENRI MATISSE

# MY MOST CREATIVE MOMENT

I served as a public-school principal for sixteen years. During that time, I earned a master of science degree in secondary education and a doctor of education in school administration. My plan was to someday become a superintendent of schools.

However, the superintendent of the school where I was a principal did not welcome staff members to school board meetings. If I had gone to a board meeting, he would have asked me what I was doing there. Then he would have told me to go on home, and he would tell me what happened at a later date.

Therefore, when I became superintendent, I had never attended a board meeting or seen a board agenda. I did get some general ideas of the proceedings from a neighboring superintendent.

At my first board meeting, I was aware that the officers of the board included a president, a vice president, and a secretary. I thought the job of the secretary was to take the minutes. The meeting was progressing well. We were following the agenda, with items passing with a motion, a second, and a vote.

We were more than halfway through the agenda when the board secretary said to me, "You *are* taking the minutes of this meeting, aren't you?" This was a shock. Why wouldn't the board secretary take the minutes? However, I did not want to admit lack of knowledge to the board, so I said, "Yes, of course!"

My most creative moment occurred the next morning when I wrote the minutes of a three-hour meeting from memory. I counted on the board members not to read the minutes or remember who made what motion or second to the different board agenda items. It worked. I became an "expert" at taking minutes of a meeting from that time forward.

*Getting better involves making hard choices.*
– UNKNOWN

# A MULTIMILLIONAIRE
# WITHOUT MILK

IN 1960, WE PURCHASED A RANCH SOUTHEAST OF
Killeen, Texas. It was used as a working cattle ranch
until 1963, when I was elected superintendent of schools
at Lampasas, Texas, about thirty miles west of Killeen.
At that time, we moved to Lampasas, leased the ranch
for cattle grazing, and sold the house and twenty acres
of land.

This arrangement continued until the early 1980s,
when we sold that ranch to a corporation with part of
the agreement making me one-fourth partner in the
corporation. The plan was designed to divide the four-
hundred-acre ranch into smaller lots. A part of the
agreement with the corporation was that they make a
down payment on a ranch in west Texas and pay the
balance over a four-year period. The corporation planned
to make payments on the west Texas ranch as lots were
sold. The ranch in west Texas was fifteen hundred acres,

with live water and excellent deer and turkey hunting. This was great, with the exception that we would not truly own the ranch until the corporation paid off the note in four years.

The corporation borrowed two million dollars to be used for developing paved streets, utility facilities, as well as other demands for a development. A large housing-development firm purchased 133 lots of the 1,400 surveyed. This sounded great; however, they did not pay for the lot until a house was built. Then they paid for the lot plus accrued interest. Everything went well until the economic crunch came in the mid-1980s, when savings-and-loan organizations and banks were going under. The obligation of the corporation was to make a $96,000 payment each year on the ranch. My part of the payment was almost $35,000 each year. When you owe two million dollars, it is next to impossible to borrow any more funds during an economic crunch no matter how big your future profits might be.

By then, I had retired and was doing consultant work. The Halls' cash flow was a massive problem. The last ranch payment took almost all of our assets. I took a job as a superintendent in the Houston area at that time. The family did not follow me to the new job. With limited funds available, I rented a small apartment, and for at least two months, my breakfast, lunch, and dinner consisted of dry cereal. For a portion of the time, I only had money to purchase the cereal but not the milk. You might be surprised to learn that when you are hungry enough, water over cereal is not half bad. So this is my story of a millionaire without milk.

Over a period of time, the cash-flow situation eased, and milk was added to my poor-boy diet. This was a good lesson for our two sons. However, I never told them about the experience until years later.

Over a twenty-year period, we had invested in real estate which in time provided an excellent return. In the late 1970s, we built our net worth to over two million dollars. However, when the economic crunch took half, we realized we had real estate but with limited cash.

*Things which matter the most must never be at*
*the mercy of things which matter the least.*
– GOETHE

# TWENTY-SEVEN STUDENTS

DURING THE MID-1980S, I SERVED AS SUPERINTENDENT of schools in one of the suburbs of Houston, Texas. Unemployment in the area hovered around 10 percent, and personal problems had a deep and penetrating effect on the high school-age students.

As the staff observed our high school students, they voiced a disturbing concern. Something was amiss in a number of them. It was not conduct, not absenteeism or attitude. What was it?

The counselor selected two male students and asked them if they would take part in a very personal interview. They hesitatingly agreed.

The interview revealed facts that we were not prepared for. The students told the counselors that some students were living in their cars or in vacant or abandoned houses. Here are some of the questions and answers on the personal interview:

Where do they eat? *The school serves breakfast and lunch.*

What about the evening meal? *There is always the dumpster behind McDonald's.*

What about bathing and showering? *We make sure we take PE so we can use the showers at school.*

What about spending money for gasoline and school supplies? *We tried to find part-time jobs on the weekend or after school. If that did not work out, we felt we were forced to shoplift.*

Why are you not living at home? No answer; the students would not discuss this issue.

Out of a high school enrollment of 723 students, over a period of time we discovered twenty-seven students living in cars or abandoned buildings. This fact was disturbing and even heart-wrenching. There were twenty-seven churches or religious organizations in the school district. We sent letters to each organization, asking that they send a representative to a school meeting to discuss a very important issue. Only two ministers attended the scheduled meeting. The two students were there and freely discussed their situation as well as some of their friends' living conditions.

We never knew exactly what happened after the meeting, but we surmised that the two ministers who had attended went to the other ministers and told them about the meeting. There was an awakening in the community. A number of students were invited to have Sunday meals with families, and some were invited to attend movies or ballgames as guests of other families. Some students were taken on fishing trips, and other weekend activities were included in some of the invitations. In one case, a wealthy lady who lived alone asked one of the girls to come live with her. Sometime later, this lady sent the girl to college.

All of the community activities were refreshing to observe and benefitted a number of students. However, in six months, the community and students returned to the "situation as usual" with students again living in their cars or abandoned buildings and only dreaming of what the situation might have been.

*Is it no longer safe to be a Christian in public?*
*Has America fallen that far?*
– TED CRUZ

# BEST-LAID PLANS

DURING THE 1990S, PUBLIC SCHOOLS IN TEXAS HAD TONED down from the hustle and bustle of the 1960s and 1970s. School board members had accepted the concept that the superintendent was elected by the board to run the schools, and the board had hopefully accepted the areas of responsibility outlined in the state-recommended board policies.

Occasionally, the system broke down. Most often when a new board member was elected and brought his own agenda to the board meetings did the system have difficulty operating smoothly. This would happen mostly when the new board member had a one item agenda concerning the superintendent's tenure. I had served as an educational consultant for a number of years, and I was also a member of a superintendent search firm that helped school boards search for and select superintendents.

Our firm had worked with a board in the Coastal Bend area of Texas to select a new superintendent for the district. The selected superintendent had done well, and the patrons of the district accepted and respected his leadership. After two years in the district, a minister of one of the local churches was elected to the board. From the first meeting of the board, it was apparent the minister's one item agenda was to fire the superintendent.

As the situation progressed from bad to worse, the board president contacted me for help. He asked if I would work with the old board, new board, and superintendent in an attempt to point out to the new board members the duties of the superintendent as well as the duties and limitations of the board. The board president was very concerned about the negative influence the situation was having on the school system.

It became obvious that the new board had little knowledge of school operations, school contracts, school law, and board meeting procedures. It was decided that the board president would arrange a lunch meeting to include the new board member, the superintendent, me (as a consultant), and himself. We had even planned a seating arrangement. The superintendent was to sit at one end of the table, the board president at the other end, with the new board member to the right of the president, and me on the other side.

We had selected a very popular barbecue restaurant for the meeting place. The establishment was well known for the huge Texas-size glasses of iced tea that came with each meal. During the early part of the meeting, before any formal discussion got underway, things seemed to be going in an amiable manner. As the meal progressed, the superintendent was passing a bottle of catsup to the new board member when he knocked the large glass of iced tea into the lap of the new board member. It was a direct hit in the crotch. The new board member – the minister – was quite embarrassed. He would not leave his position at the table until his clothing was completely dry. As you can imagine, our well-laid plans came crashing down on us. Although the minister never openly accused the superintendent of purposely turning over the tea, rumors spread around town that the minister had considered the possibility. The superintendent stayed for the next year and then took another position as superintendent in another school district.

*The key to being a good manager is keeping the people who hate you away from those who are still undecided.*
– CASEY STENGEL

# NO ONE KNOWS MY NAME

DURING THE TWILIGHT OF MY CAREER, I SERVED AS interim superintendent of a school district in the Houston, Texas, area. Although I was interim, I stayed in that position for eight years. During that time, the school board was made up of relatively young men and women. We developed a "special relationship," even though they considered me elderly. My service to the school was rewarding and satisfying.

Almost every day when I left the office, I stopped at a grocery store to secure needed commodities. Because of my frequent shopping at the store, I developed a friendship with a young man who was employed as a sack boy there. I always looked forward to my short visit and kidding with him.

I later learned he was a student at one of the high schools in my district. I wondered why I seldom saw him on my regular visits to the high school. Then one day, I heard he had withdrawn from school.

Upon my next visit to the grocery store, he was there doing his job as sack boy. I inquired as to the story I had heard, which he confirmed was true. I asked why and asked if I could help.

His reply took me by surprise and hit home at my profession. His reply was, "You are the only one up there who knows my name."

*Dropouts make up most of the nation's prison inmates.*
*About 75 percent of America's state prison inmates,*
*almost 59 percent of federal inmates, and 69 percent of*
*local jail inmates did not complete high school.*
– UNKNOWN

# CHECKING SPEED WITH A HIGHWAY PATROLMAN

DURING THE LATE 1980S AND PART OF THE 1990S, I WAS the superintendent of a school district in the Houston area. Most weekends, I drove about 180 miles north on Interstate 10 to Seguin to stay at our retirement home on Lake McQueeney.

This was during the time when highway speeds in Texas were fifty-five miles an hour. This 180-mile distance covered many miles of sparsely populated areas, with only a few towns along the way. Much of my time on the road was late at night or very early in the morning. Because of this, I often caught myself driving over the speed limit.

One of our school board members was a highway patrolman. I asked him how strict the members of the patrol were in enforcing the fifty-five-mile speed limit during late-night and early-morning hours. His reply was that veteran patrol members would consider the circumstances, but the younger officers would probably enforce the speed limit to the letter of the law.

After some discussion, he told me the first thing that needed to be done was to check the speedometer on my car for accuracy. He volunteered to come to my office after school one day so we could go to a county road and check the speedometer.

As planned, we went to a county road where the patrolman instructed me to get my speed up to fifty-five. When I reached that speed, I was to signal to him. At that point, I would maintain the speed for about a mile while he clocked me. Then he would turn on the patrol lights to let me know the test had been completed. During the test, we met an oncoming car, so we decided to do the same test going the opposite direction. This time, the test carried us by the high school football practice field. So, we did another test, repeating the same procedure. Once the patrolman was satisfied with the test, he turned on his patrol car lights to signal that the test was over.

The next day, I had business at the high school. As I entered the building, two football players approached me. They said, "Hey, Doc, we thought you were going to outrun that highway patrol! We were pulling for you."

The next time I saw the patrolman, I told him that we should repeat the speedometer test every six weeks or so because when the students thought I was attempting to outrun the patrolman, my status was greatly improved.

*Public opinion is an awesome assessment*
*from which there is no appeal.*
– UNKNOWN

# NO TICKET FOR SPEEDING
# AT YOUR AGE

During the 1990s, I served as superintendent of Huffman Public Schools, which is located on the east side of Lake Houston. Early one morning, I was on my way to an educational meeting in Houston. My route took me through the city of Humble. Where I entered the city, the highway went over a viaduct.

As I topped the crest of the viaduct, I saw a police car parked on the side of the road. I was exceeding the speed limit, so as I passed the police car, the officer followed me with his lights flashing. I proceeded off the viaduct and stopped in a parking lot. The officer followed the procedure of asking if there was an emergency, and he requested my driver's license. He returned to his patrol car, and in about five minutes, he returned to my side of the car. His question surprised me. It was one of the few times I appreciated my age of eighty-one. He asked, "Are you as old as is indicated on your driver's license?"

I replied, "Yes, sir." Next, he asked the purpose of the trip. I told him I was the superintendent of the Huffman School System and I was on my way to an educational meeting in Houston.

He replied, "Are you still working? You are certainly old enough to retire."

I told him I had retired some years ago but found that retirement was not what it was supposed to be. I need the working salary to get by.

He told me, "Okay, Mr. Hall, I am not going to give a ticket to anyone as old as you are and still working. I will soon be up for retirement, and I will remember this conversation."

*Old people like to give good advice as solace for no longer being able to provide bad examples.*
– ROCHEFOUCAULD

# A DELAYED HUG

One of the mysteries of school administrators is what environment the individual students have been exposed to before entering a school year.

During the early 2000s, I have served as superintendent of a group of charter schools in Texas. On one occasion, I attended a high school graduation. As the exercise ended, each graduate's name was called when the principal handed the student his or her diploma. The principal hugged each girl and boy.

I observed one male graduate to be almost six feet tall and probably one hundred seventy pounds. He was a good-looking young man. After he had been hugged by the principal, he walked off the stage and said, "That is the first time I been hugged since I was in fourth grade."

*Treat a person as he is, and he will remain as he is.*
*Treat him as he could be, and he will become what he should be.*
– JIMMY JOHNSON

# CARDBOARD FOR DINNER

I WILL NEVER FORGET HELEN (NOT HER REAL NAME). SHE was a tenth-grade student at one of the charter schools we operated. One day, after Helen had eaten lunch in the lunchroom, she complimented the lady who worked there by telling her how much she had enjoyed the meal. This is unusual, since a positive statement from students about the food in the lunchroom is rare. Then Helen passed on a bit of knowledge she learned from being homeless: if you are homeless and you are hungry, you can eat cardboard and drink water. It causes the cardboard to swell and give you a feeling of fullness.

When I met Helen, I was impressed with her attractive smile. However, I was startled by the expression in her eyes. Her eyes were sad, with a faraway look of loneliness. She had been placed in tenth grade because of her age and the lack of school records. She presented herself in a pleasing manner and appeared to be interested in school and her surroundings.

We learned that Helen's mother was serving time in prison and that the whereabouts of her father were unknown. Little was known about Helen's past or how long she had been homeless. Although she sometimes stayed at the Red Cross shelter, she was unable to stay there every night because there was a nominal fee charged each night and Helen did not always have the funds to pay.

The school staff and student body accepted Helen and extended hands of friendship to her. I was told she wanted to become a nurse. The staff at the school was committed to supporting Helen in making her plan a reality and did. She graduated from high school and went on to further her education.

*Sometimes courage is the quiet voice at the end of the day saying "I will try again tomorrow."*
– UNKNOWN

# GUILTY: NOT RECOGNIZING KIDS' CRIES FOR HELP

AT AGE NINETY-FOUR, I AM OFTEN ASKED WHY I AM STILL actively engaged in the field of education. I serve as superintendent of a charter school system with ten campuses located throughout Texas. I am in good health, with ample energy and a strong desire to help young people as they grow toward adulthood.

I do not respond in truth to those inquiries about the why of my continuing in this profession. The real reason is guilt. I am trying to pay back for all the years I served as a teacher, principal, and superintendent and did not recognize a student's cry for help.

I was a strong disciplinarian and made few exceptions to a strict interpretation of the school policies and requirements. Now, I realize that often behavior or noncompliance to rules and regulations might have been a student's way to be recognized.

I recall talking with a student who had shown

disrespect to a teacher followed by the destruction of school property. My statement to him was, "What would your dad think if he knew about your conduct in this situation?" His response should have given me a clue to his problem when he answered, "Mr. Hall, I wish I thought he would care!"

I have been guilty of paying little attention to cries for help or recognition from students. So many times, I received a signal of need for help, and I did not respond.

Today, I am not working directly with each student in all ten schools, but I am providing mentoring and support to the teachers and principals at each school. I have approved students' trips, Thanksgiving meals, and many other activities at the schools to promote the students' belonging and feelings of worthiness. When student issues are brought to me, I approach each situation with a great deal of consideration and interest. Today, I am searching for the students and teachers I can help travel down the pathway to success.

*I am only one, but I am one. I cannot do*
*everything, but I can do something.*
*And I will not let what I cannot do interfere with what I can do.*
– REVEREND EDWARD EVERETT HALE

# Things I Have Learned

The learning experiences of a long life can be varied and many. Fortunately, most of mine have been related to the humorous side of my profession and lifestyle.

*When you reread a classic you do not see more in the book than*
*you did before; you see more in you than there was before.*
 – CLIFTON FADIMAN

# AS TIME GOES BY

WHEN ADVANCED AGE FORCES YOU TO REALIZE THE ultimate approaching calumniation of a lifetime, your thoughts race back over rarely used memory lanes, crossing trails long ago forgotten.

*Clarity affects focus.*
– THOMAS LEONARD

# BROKEN FUTURES

As a school principal, I never realized where many students come from until I learned that many must be handled with care because most of their world involves only things that were broken.

*Gratitude is riches. Complaint is poverty.*
– DORIS DAY

# THE BEST COMPLIMENT
# I EVER HAD

ONE OF THE MANY REAL PLEASURES I ENJOYED DURING the later years of my lifetime was associating with all walks of life—the rich, the poor, the browns, the blacks, the whites, the haves and the have-nots, and all of the in-betweens. I placed myself in their position and enjoyed the relationships.

The best compliment I ever had was on an occasion when I was enjoying visiting with a mixed group. One individual said to me, "Norm, you are wealthy; you just make out like you are poor."

*It's easy to make a buck. It's a lot tougher to make a difference.*
– TOM BROKAW

# PRUNE JUICE

DURING A LARGE PART OF MY PROFESSIONAL LIFE, I traveled extensively, fulfilling speaking engagements throughout the lower forty-eight states, Canada, and Mexico. The one thing I always dreaded was the possibility of catching the flu or even a cold.

I was sitting in a bar one night and commented to the bartender that I might be coming down with the flu. I had been coughing and sneezing and seemed to have a slight fever. He turned away from me, selected a small glass, filled it with a dark liquid, and passed it to me.

"What is that?" I asked.

He replied, "Prune juice."

I said, "I did not know prune juice was good for the flu!"

He said, "I don't know about that, but I tell you one thing: you will think twice before you cough."

*Try and fail.*
*Don't fail to try.*
– UNKNOWN

# A REFEREE GONE SOUTH

I coached basketball for a number of years and then for a period of some nine years, I refereed games.

I stopped refereeing for two reasons: 1. My eyesight decreased. 2. My hearing improved.

*Reliable technology requires:*
- *The right people*
- *The right training*
- *The right support*
- *The right platform*
- *The right delivery*

– UNKNOWN

# STEALING YOUR TOMORROW

With the exception of four years in the army, I spent my entire professional life as a teacher or administrator in the public schools of Texas. I took great pride and pleasure in observing the students as they grew and developed into adulthood. I witnessed some disappointments and many pleasant and predictable outcomes.

I was often puzzled by what influenced students. Over a period of time, I came to believe that one phrase seemed to have a great impact on the majority of students as they began to reach adulthood. I told many students: don't let something steal your tomorrows.

A lesson learned.

*Graduating from high school will determine how well one lives for the next fifty years of their life. High school graduates earn $143 more per week than high school dropouts (and college graduates earn $479 more per week).*
– UNKNOWN

# YOUNG PEOPLE AND THE ELDERLY

As I grew up, I was taught to be respectful of the elderly. I learned to be courteous, helpful, and sensitive to their needs. As I spent a career in the field of education, I learned another valuable lesson that I did not understand for a number of years.

The lesson: young people can be as lonely as the elderly.

*Personality has the power to uplift, power to depress, power to curse, and power to bless.*
– PAUL HARRIS

# JUDGING CHARACTER

YOU CAN EASILY JUDGE THE CHARACTER OF OTHERS BY how they treat those who they think can do nothing for them.

People will forget what you said.

People will forget what you did.

But people will never forget how you made them feel.

*People don't care how much you know until*
*they find out how much you care.*
– UNKNOWN

# THE MIDDLE AGE TEST

As a man grows older, he sometimes wonders if he has reached middle age. There is a surefire test that will remove any doubt about if and when you have reached middle age.

The test is if you do not care where your wife goes at night, as long as you don't have to go with her, then you have reached middle age.

*Baseball is 90 percent mental, and the other half is physical.*
– YOGI BERRA

# FOOD FOR THOUGHT

As of July 2016, one out of every forty-five children – some 1.6 million – is homeless in the United States. Most of these children are under the age of seven.

- Keep in mind, a youth can be as lonely as an elderly person.
- Children age three to six laugh over twenty-six times a day, while adults laugh an average of barely fifteen times a day.
- Success is often on the far side of failure.
- Success is most often made from a number of failures.
- You can get almost anything you want in life if you will help enough other people get what they want.

- Competition is a powerful tool in the game of life—for about forty hours. After that, competition drops off substantially.

*There is no "I" in team.*

– UNKNOWN

# FASCINATION OF AN ATTITUDE

As I went through school, a number of individuals became my role models. One in particular was Bobby Lane, who played quarterback for the University of Texas. He went on to have an exceptional career in professional football with the National Football League.

My fascination with him was based on his exceptional attitude. He made a statement a number of times that expressed his philosophy regarding winning and losing. He often said, "I never lost a ballgame; I just ran out of time."

*Ability is what you're capable of doing.*
*Motivation determines what you do.*
*Attitude determines how well you do it.*
– LOU HOLTZ

# A RULE OF THUMB TO LIVE BY

Do not be dismayed at an occasional defeat.

For without them, your victories would be such hollow chambers.

*Planning means understanding content, learning styles,*
*pacing, sequencing, and what success looks like.*
– UNKNOWN

# THE WORST THING ABOUT GROWING OLD

A friend asked me, "Do you know what the worst thing about growing old is?"

I replied, "No, what is it?"

He replied, "Growing old!"

After passing my ninetieth birthday, I agree.

*Always go to other people's funerals;*
*otherwise they won't come to yours.*
— YOGI BERRA

# Travel

Travel was a large part of our lifestyle. Billye enjoyed travel with an adventurous spirit. We visited over one hundred foreign countries. We went behind Russia's iron curtain a number of times. The Caribbean and the South Seas provided many meaningful experiences.

*Travelers are always discoverers, especially those
who travel by air. There are no signposts in the sky
to show a man has passed that way before.*
– ANNE M. LINDBERGH

# THE SWITCHBLADE

DURING THE MID-1970S, OUR FAMILY VISITED RUSSIA. Billye had reservations about the trip. So, when we left New York on the way to Amsterdam and on to Moscow, I commented to Billye, "The plane is almost full, so a lot of people must be going to Russia."

When the plane left Amsterdam on the way to Moscow, there were only eleven people and the crew on the plane. Five of the eleven were in the Hall group.

The plane landed in Moscow and remained out in the field area since it had no loading ramps. A bus came out to the plane to pick up the passengers. As we loaded onto the bus, the motor died. Several of the passengers got out of the bus and pushed it until it started.

Billye had told Charlie not to carry his switchblade pocketknife with him. This was a time when the switchblades were " all the go" in the United States. Charlie's interpretation of this directive was not to carry it on his person, but in the luggage would be permissible.

Charlie was the first to go through customs, and, of course, they found the knife. The customs agent, not knowing about switchblades, was trying to open the knife when Charlie came to his aid. Charlie was delighted to demonstrate how the switchblade opened and closed. This created quite a show in the Moscow airport. The customs agent called other agents over and demonstrated how the knife worked. Several agents had to try out the new device.

Billye and I were nervously awaiting the outcome of this event. But in the end, they returned the knife to Charlie, closed his luggage, and motioned him on. The agent turned to Billye and me and asked if we were with Charlie. When we replied yes, he motioned us on through the checkpoint without checking our luggage.

*I don't want to waste time learning what I already know.*
– RICHARD MILBURN ACADEMY STUDENT

# INSIDE THE COLD WAR

ON A SECOND TRIP TO RUSSIA DURING THE LATE 1970S, we experienced a problem leaving the country. Billye's passport picture had been taken when she had long hair. In the meantime, she had her hair cut in a rather short style.

All went well during our two-week tour of Moscow and the surrounding area, including extended trips to St. Petersburg, Smolemar, and Daugmipiler. However, upon our scheduled departure from the Moscow airport, a problem developed. In those days, there were no covered ramps from the terminal to the plane door. Planes were parked just off the runway from the terminal, and buses carried the passengers to the designated planes. We boarded the bus and were driven to our plane. Passengers were lined up for a pre-boarding inspection. There were no ticket windows. Instead, there was an interview with an officer who asked questions and examined the passport. When it was Billye's turn to interview, the officer noticed her short hair compared to her passport picture with long hair. He called another officer to join him. They continued with the questions. All this time, the line of passengers was being held up. Another officer of rank was called to join the conference. At this time, they pulled Billye out of line to allow the other passengers to board the plane.

I was faced with a dilemma at this time: Should I stay in Russia with Billye or, because the plane was bound for Paris, should I go to France to secure help from the American Embassy? At this time, a female officer drove up in a staff car and took over the proceedings. She asked Billye questions concerning why and when she had the haircut. Finally, the lady officer told Billye that she understood, and Billye was finally allowed to board the aircraft.

The incident made a lasting impression on both of us. It increased an already deep appreciation and love for having been born in the good old United States of America.

*We hold these truths to be self-evident, that all men are created equal, that they are endowed by their Creator with certain unalienable Rights, that among these are Life, Liberty and pursuit of Happiness.*
– THE DECLARATION OF INDEPENDENCE, 1776

# THE ALLENBY BRIDGE

IN THE SUMMER OF 1986, MY FAMILY AND I TOOK A TOUR of Europe during which we were to cross over the Allenby Bridge, which crossed over the Jordan River and the West Bank. We were aware of the conflict between the two countries because of the news coverage in the United States, so we were not surprised to see troops stationed on each side of the bridge as we began to cross. Before we were allowed to cross the bridge, we were taken to a building that served as a check station where passports and luggage were carefully examined.

As the luggage was being examined, the custom officer saw my son Charlie's cowboy boots. The officer called for the supervisor, who seemed fascinated with the boots. He asked Charlie a number of questions. Then the supervisor began to try on the boots with some difficulty. Charlie was more than glad to help in the process. After getting the boots on, the supervisor walked around the lobby area, modeling the boots. He called attention to the boots to other members of the customs group.

While the other members of our tour waited, two other members of the customs group tried on the boots. They, too, paraded around the lobby area. I told my wife we may lose a pair of boots, but it would be worth it if we were granted passage.

Finally, the customs group returned to business and returned the boots to Charlie, who was cleared by customs. When it was our turn to go through customs, the officer asked if we were Charlie's parents. When we said yes, we were passed through without our luggage being inspected.

*Freedom breeds freedom. Nothing else does.*
– ANNE ROE

# OUT TO SEA IN A CANOE

DURING THE SUMMER OF 1998, BILLYE, CHARLIE, AND I were on the island of Bali in the South Pacific as members of a tour group. Bali was a small but beautiful island with long, sandy beaches and tree-covered hills. There were two modern hotels on the island located some two miles apart. All along the east side of the island was a coral reef, which was fifty yards from the island proper.

Billye and I walked along the beach from our hotel to the other one. After exploring the area around the second hotel, we decided to return to ours. As we started our return trip down the beach to our hotel, we noticed a number of canoes along the beach and were told that they made trips back and forth between the two hotels. I suggested to Billye that we take the canoe back to our hotel. She agreed, provided we stayed between the island and the coral reef.

When we started our trip, one native was in the

front of the canoe, and the other was in the back. Each native had a paddle. As we started, we noticed the tide was going out, which caused the canoe to run aground several times in a short period of time. One native approached me and asked about getting outside the coral reef to finish our trip. Reluctantly, Billye agreed. Thus, we moved to the ocean side of the coral reef.

Things went well for a while. The two natives were singing and appeared to be in a gay mood. However, in a short period of time, the water grew rough, and the natives had to move the canoe further away from the coral reef to keep from being slammed into it. As a part of the tourist trade, a passageway had been blasted through the coral formation to allow boats and canoes passage to the two hotels. As we approached the passage leading to our hotel, the sea became so rough that it pushed us away from the entry through the reef. This caused the natives to row away from the reef and back off to try another entry. The waves were exceedingly high! As we were pushed further out into the Indian Ocean, the waves were some fifteen feet high. However, our dugout canoe rode the waves with no trouble.

What we did not know was that we were involved in an earthquake. As the natives battled to return to the passage through the reef, we noticed a yacht attempting to ride the wave a mile or so away. The yacht would appear to be almost on its side and then reappear, only to go out of sight again. Finally, it disappeared from sight altogether.

At last, the sea calmed to some extent, and we were able to get through the passage to the island proper. It was only then that we were told about the earthquake. Five hundred forty-two people died as a result of this quake. When we returned to the hotel, we found the mirrors and windows in our room cracked, and the items on the bathroom counter were scattered on the floor. Many tourists had to sleep on the tennis court that night because of damage to their rooms. Charlie, who had gone with a group to visit a coconut plantation, said the danger there was the coconuts falling from the trees and the ground shaking so that it was hard to walk or stand.

With this event, we learned what people on the islands of the South Pacific experience from time to time.

*Be it ever so humble, there's no place like home.*
– JOHN HOWARD PAYNE

# Stories I Like to Tell

Stories that live on in one's life can have a deep meaning and significance, be a tie to the past, or measure the humor in one's life. In my case, it is a combination of the three.

*Copy success.*
– UNKNOWN

# A DOG AND CAT STORY

TRUE LAUGHTER IS A CURE-ALL FOR ALMOST ANY occasion. I have a friend who tells this joke.

A man, wife, and their eight-year-old son lived in a small house in a rural community. A stray dog caught the son's attention, so he asked his father if he could keep the dog. The father said, "No, son. We have no backyard, and we are not in a position to maintain a pet dog."

The son's reply was "Can I sell him?"

The father's reply was "Yes, if you can find a buyer."

The next day, the father came home from work to find a sign in the front yard that read "Dog for sale—$1.00." The father asked the son if he had any nibbles toward the sale. The son said, "No, not one."

The father suggested that he raise the price of the dog. His idea was that an increase in price might lead people to believe the dog was more than just a stray dog.

So, the son placed a new sign in the yard. It read: "Dog for sale—$1,000."

The next day, when the father came home from work, the sign was gone. He asked his son, "Did you sell the dog?"

The boy replied, "Yes, I did."

The father said, "You mean someone gave you $1,000 for that dog?"

The son replied, "Well, not exactly. I took two $500 cats as a trade."

*The difficult is what takes a little time. The impossible is what takes a little longer.*
– FRIDTJOF NANSEN

# FOOTBALL MADE EASY

During the times before Fort Hood was established in west Bell County, Texas, the town of Killeen was the marketplace for an area made up of ranches and farms. The town population was twelve hundred, plus or minus a few. The school system had an enrollment of 325, more or less, in grades one through eleven. Football and baseball were the popular sports. With no paved roads and a party-line telephone system, people lived almost in isolation.

I recall a story told around the school and town concerning one of the students who entered school in Killeen. It seemed that the boy had been going to one of the country schools in the area before he came to the Killeen school to enroll. The country schools were usually two-teacher schools that included grades one through seven. After seventh grade, the student would transfer to the Killeen school.

The prospective student had ridden his horse to school, which was not an unusual practice at the time. After the first week of school, the boy – Earl Cole – got on his horse and headed home. He rode by the football field, where the team was practicing. After seeing him sitting on his horse to observe the team practice, the football coach called out to him, "Some of the team members tell me you might be interested in coming out for football."

Earl replied, "Coach, I don't know anything about the game. I have never even seen the game played."

In response, the coach said, "There is nothing to it. I will pitch the ball to you, and then you run through the first group you see there and then run on up the field and cross the goal line."

Earl took off doing just what the coach had outlined. He ran through the first group of players, then on through the second group, and crossed the goal line.

Earl came back to the coach and said, "Coach, how was that?"

The coach replied, "Say, that was pretty good. Now get off your horse and try it."

*Coaching means taking part in professional*
*dialogue with leadership and peers.*
*It also means being a coach as well as accepting a coach.*
– UNKNOWN

# SMALL THINGS FIRST

DURING WORLD WAR II, ONE OF MY FELLOW OFFICERS was on patrol in the Philippine Islands when his patrol came under enemy fire. This caused his men to search for cover. During the exchange of fire, he and a sergeant became separated from the other patrol members.

As the battle wore on, he and the sergeant seemed to be singled out and pursued by the enemy. They went from cover to cover, trying to elude the Japanese. Finally, as darkness approached, the two found refuge behind a large rock in an open clearing. Gunfire was exchanged until darkness set in. They knew they were surrounded, with little hope of escape.

As daylight came the next day, they decided to make a desperate attempt to escape. They checked their rifles and brushed their teeth. As they moved from the cover of the rock, they were prepared to attempt to shoot their way to the cover of the jungle. There was no gunfire as they raced to the jungle. Several hours later, they were able to rejoin their company.

I have always wondered about their last activity before they made the desperate run for freedom. They used the last of the water in their canteens to brush their teeth!

*The thing that cowardice fears most is decision.*
– SOREN KIERKEGAARD

# FISHING WITH A
# TELEPHONE LINE

BRANTLY WAS ON ONE OF THE KILLEEN FOOTBALL TEAMS I coached in the late 1940s. After high school, he remained in Killeen, married, and started a family. Even though Brantly and his wife were hard workers, Brantly was never accepted by his father-in-law.

In time, the father-in-law, who was military, retired in Killeen. Even with the three grandchildren, he never attempted to accept Brantly. Because of the father-in-law's love of fishing, Brantly and his wife came up with a plan they felt would cause the father-in-law to admire and respect Brantly. He and his friends had been very successful using a new fishing technique that he planned to share with his father-in-law. This illegal method of fishing consisted of hooking up a wire line to a telephone that used a crank to sound rings. The line was placed into the water, and the old-style crank phone was cranked as though one were ringing the phone. This caused current to flow through the water, resulting in many fish coming to the surface of the river where they could easily be caught in a hand net.

The father-in-law agreed to go on the planned fishing trip to the Lampasas River. They proceeded to place the line into the water and crank the telephone. The system worked! The fish came to the surface. The father-in-law was excited to begin netting the fish and placing them into the boat.

All was going well. The relationship even seemed to be warming. There was even a noticeable degree of conversation. And then along came the game warden. Brantly and his father-in-law were fined $190 each. There has been no record of any improvement in the relationship between the two men since the fishing trip.

*Ever notice how "What the hell?" is always the right answer?*
– MARILYN MONROE

# LIGHT HUMOR

About the fifth time a man was picked up for speeding, the judge thought he needed to learn more about the man.

The judge asked the man, "Are your neighbors honest?"

The man said, "Yes, they are."

The judge said, "I understand you keep a loaded shotgun by your back door to protect your henhouse. If they are honest, why do you do that?"

The man said, "That is what keeps them honest."

*The best ambassador is a warship.*
– ADMIRAL MICHELLE HOWARD

# THE CURB

WE ONCE LIVED NEXT DOOR TO NEIGHBORS WHO WERE the parents of a three-year-old son named Tommy. During Tommy's earlier years, he had been confined to the fenced backyard. There he could play on the swing set, ride his tricycle, and chase his dog.

When Tommy reached three-plus years of age, his mother took him to the front yard and instructed him not to go past the curb. Within ten minutes, his mother saw that he had crossed the curb and was standing on the side of the street. She rushed to his side, picked him up, and returned him to his yard. She told him again that he was not to go past the curb. Another ten minutes passed, and Tommy was again past the curb and standing near the street. His mother was horrified and rushed to bring him back into the yard with a firm warning not to go beyond the curb. Within fifteen minutes, Tommy was again beyond the curb and on the side of the street.

This time, his mother returned him to the yard with a spanking and another statement of "Tommy, I have told you three times to not go beyond the curb."

Through the crying and tears, Tommy asked, "Mother, what is the curb?"

*Education does not cost. It pays.*
– UNKNOWN

# PROPERTY OWNERSHIP

Aubry Ray was born and raised in Killeen, Texas. He went to school there, and as he grew to manhood, he joined the Texas National Guard. During his tenure in the guard, he took part in the training exercises, including shooting on the rifle range.

During the early 1930s, he left Killeen and made a name for himself as a bank robber. He was sent to the state prison twice but managed to escape each time. He became a hunted man.

On one occasion, it was rumored that he was in the Killeen area. One morning in early July, Aubry Ray drove up to the Killeen Armory headquarters, which was located near the fire station in downtown Killeen. He broke the lock on the front door of the headquarters and entered. Across the street in Gary's Hardware Store, a group of people were observing Aubry's activities. Among the group was Jim Evans, who was a captain in the National

Guard unit. J. C. Woods, who was the mayor of Killeen, was also present.

Soon, Aubry returned to his car carrying three Springfield rifles, two forty-five-caliber automatic pistols, army blankets, and several boxes of ammunition.

J. C. Woods said to Jim Evans, "Aren't you going to do something? He is taking property that belongs to the government."

Jim Evans replied, "It is as much your property as it is mine! Why don't you do something?"

Aubry Ray left Killeen unchallenged for his activities.

*Half the lies they tell about me aren't true.*
– YOGI BERRA

# THE CHIMNEY AND INDIANS

DURING THE SECOND HALF OF THE NINETEENTH century, early settlers in central Texas had a common practice of driving their cattle west to more fertile grasslands for the winter months. This grass was thicker, taller, and higher in nutrients. By moving the cattle west, the winters were not as severe for the livestock.

Indians were still active at this time in western Texas where the ranchers were driving the cattle for the winter. My great-grandfather was one of a group of ranchers who drove the herd west from the land that is now the communities of Killeen, Copperas Cove, and Gatesville. Several of the ranchers built cabins out west with chimneys that were larger than usual. In fact, they were large enough for a man to crawl up inside. The ranchers also put steps inside the chimney, which provided a secure spot for a person to crawl up inside the chimney. From the chimney top, the rancher could observe the terrain around the cabin, thus enabling him to prevent a possible Indian ambush as he exited the cabin.

*The greatest accomplishment is not in never failing, but in rising again after you fall.*
– VINCE LOMBARDI

# EASY-TO-GET-TO HIP POCKETS

WHILE LIVING IN KILLEEN, TEXAS, THERE WAS A TIME when I served as a lay leader of my church. One of the duties of such a position was to preside occasionally at the church service.

One July, our church scheduled what is known as a revival. This usually meant a large tent was set up on a vacant lot and a visiting minister was invited to preach each night for a week or ten days. People from all denominations usually attended. On this occasion, an elderly but well-known and effective minister was invited to conduct the revival.

On the first night after the visiting minister had given a well-received message, I announced that a certain song would follow; after the song, I asked the congregation to be seated. Once they were seated, I said the ushers would come forward and pass among the congregation to collect the offering.

After the service was over, the visiting minister

approached me and said he would like to offer a suggestion to me concerning presiding over the church service. His suggestion was: never take a church offering while the congregation was seated. If the offering is taken while they are standing, the men can get to the billfold in their hip pockets much more easily.

*If you can't start a meeting on time, start it early.*
– GALE BARTOW

# ANOTHER CAT

Jᴉᴍ Lᴀɴɢᴇ ᴡᴀs ᴀ ᴄʜᴇᴍɪsᴛʀʏ ᴛᴇᴀᴄʜᴇʀ ᴀᴛ Sᴇɢᴜɪɴ Hɪɢʜ School during the 1970s and 1980s. His pet cat had a bountiful litter of kittens. He asked my grandson – Randy –to take one of the kittens, which he did.

As time went on, Jim had a problem giving the kittens away. Still later, he gave a chemistry test at the high school. Randy was not a scholar in chemistry by any means, even though his other grades were good and he had been invited to join the National Honor Society. When the test was returned, written in red across the top of the test was "By my good grace, your grade is 70. How about another cat?"

*Next in importance to freedom and justice is*
*popular education, without which neither freedom*
*nor justice can be permanently maintained.*
– JAMES A. GARFIELD

# A CUT-RATE DONATION

A MEMBER OF MY CHURCH WHO WAS SOMEWHAT conservative was attending a Sunday morning church service with his family. At the end of the service, when the collection plate was passed for donations, the conservative member fumbled in his billfold and by mistake placed a twenty-dollar bill in the plate. After realizing what he had done, he was very upset.

He wondered if he went to the back of the church and explained his mistake to the usher if he might be able to retrieve his twenty-dollar bill. His wife told him, "No way!" Then he reasoned that at the end of the service, he would go to the pastor's office and explain the situation to the pastor and possibly retrieve his twenty-dollar bill. To this his wife again said, "No!"

As the church service moved into the call for new members, announcements, and then to the final prayer, the conservative member decided to let the twenty dollars go and take pride in his offering.

Upon hearing his decision, his wife commented, "Well, you may let the twenty dollars go, but heaven is only going to give you credit for one dollar because that is all you intended to give."

*It don't bother me what people know. What does bother me is what people know that just plain ain't so.*
– WILL ROGERS

# ROUNDING UP CATTLE
# ON A MOTORCYCLE

WHILE I WAS LIVING IN WEST TEXAS, I HAD A NEIGHBOR who was a very successful rancher. He was perhaps sixty-plus years old but still young at heart.

Upon one occasion, when he went to one of his ranch sites riding his motorcycle, he decided to round up some of the cattle (place them in a stock pen).

Although it is not recommended to round up cattle on a motorcycle, a few ranchers have tried it. Such an activity requires quick turns and sudden stops, along with varying rates of speed. During a burst of speed followed by a quick turn, the rancher lost his balance, and the motorcycle turned over.

Realizing he had broken his ankle, he had to make a plan on how to get home. He was about three miles off a road, so he knew it would be a long time before someone found him. (This was before the days when the cell phone became so popular.) He decided the only solution was to right the motorcycle and ride it to the main entrance of his ranch. He knew local residents traveled that paved road, and he would be found.

He was able to right the cycle, get on, get it started, and head toward the ranch entrance. He had forgotten that the broken ankle was on the same side as the cycle brake, and he could not stop the cycle! He ran through the gate entrance and crashed on the other side of the paved road.

In due time, a neighbor saw the accident and notified the rancher's wife. In about two hours, the rancher's sons-in-law arrived in a pickup truck. They were prepared to rescue the rancher and take the motorcycle home.

Later, my neighbor told me that was one of the few times he was glad to see his sons-in-law.

*Those who expect to reap the blessings of freedom must,*
*like men, undergo the fatigue of supporting it.*
– THOMAS PAINE

# AGGIES' KISSING TRADITION

FOR YEARS, THE TEXAS AGGIE TRADITION AT FOOTBALL games has been that when the Aggie team makes a touchdown, the Aggie gets to kiss his date. Often, when a score is made by the Aggies, the sports broadcasters will scan the stands with the TV camera, exposing many Aggies caught in the act.

A young lady told me about her experience with an Aggie on their first date. When she was a high school senior, she was invited to attend a football game with an A&M student. As the game progressed, Texas A&M scored a touchdown, whereupon the Aggie kissed her in a warm embrace. She explained that her first thought was concern about her mother seeing her kissing the young man during the TV broadcast. She went on to explain that her concern mounted as the game progressed. The Aggies won the game fifty-six to six.

*Life is what happens to you when you're busy making other plans.*
– JOHN LENNON

# WAITING ON THE FLOWER SEEDS

DURING MY YEARS IN COLLEGE, I DEVELOPED A friendship with a boy from Seguin, Texas. He was an excellent student who later established a successful career in civil engineering. In fact, he became the state highway engineer and worked as head of the Texas Highway Department.

At that time, one of the duties of the highway department was to provide flower seeds to different areas of the state. One year, the highway department had filled all the requests for flower seeds and had five cans remaining. I asked if I could have the extra seeds. I was told yes. I should come by the department and pick up the cans.

Two weeks later, I went by the department to pick up the seeds. I was told that only one can remained. I asked about the missing cans and was told that the governor had requested four cans.

With tongue in cheek, I asked, "How come the governor gets four cans and I only get one?"

I thought the state highway engineer gave an excellent answer: "Hall, when you get to be governor, you can have four cans of flower seeds."

It has been thirty-two years, and I still have not gotten the four cans of flower seeds.

*As you make decisions, take the time to let the logical side of your brain "kick in."*
– UNKNOWN

# PUT THE HAT BACK ON

WHEN BILLYE — MY WIFE — WAS A BABY, HER MOTHER decided to have her picture made. Billye's mother had a difficult time arranging Billye's hair to her satisfaction that day. After experiencing little success, she decided to have Billye wear a bonnet to cover her hair.

This was in the early 1930s, and Killeen was a country town of just a little over one thousand people. On the way to the photo shop, Billye and her mother had to walk past Wood's Drug Store. As usual, Dr. Wood was sitting on one of the benches on the sidewalk in front of his store.

As Billye and her mother walked past Dr. Wood, he greeted them. During the conversation, he asked where they were going. Billye's mother told him they were going to get Billye's picture made. Dr. Wood observed the bonnet and asked, "Don't you think she would look better without the bonnet?"

In response, Billye's mother removed the bonnet to

reveal the hair problem. Dr. Wood said, "My God! Put the bonnet back on!"

We still have that picture. I use it as blackmail to keep Billye in line.

*The real secret to success is enthusiasm.*
– WALTER CHRYSLER

# CAN'T TEACH AN OLD DOG NEW TRICKS

A NEW SUPERINTENDENT ASSUMED HIS POSITION ON JULY 1 in the Copperas Cove School District. The year was about 1961. Copperas Cove had not yet experienced its later phenomenal growth in population.

The new superintendent surveyed the operations of the district. As he did so, he noted a number of changes that he intended to make. One change was the janitorial service being provided at the high school. The custodian had had the responsibility for the high school for a number of years without any complaints.

Several weeks went by, and the superintendent made daily suggestions for improving the efficiency of the custodial services at the high school. The custodian would often respond to the superintendent's directive with: "You can't teach an old dog new tricks."

Finally, after hearing this reply for a number of times, the superintendent replied, "Well then, I am going to get a new dog."

*If a young male does not learn to read by seventh grade, research indicates he is likely to end up in juvenile court.*
– UNKNOWN

# HE WALKED EVERYWHERE
# HE WENT

WHILE L LIVED IN LAMPASAS, TEXAS, I HAD A NEIGHBOR who had a young son who was enrolled in the tenth grade at the local high school. He had secured his driver's license at the age of sixteen and was allowed to drive the family car from time to time and even on an occasional date.

The boy's father became unhappy with him because the son continued to let his hair grow long. During the 1970s, long hair on a male was not an acceptable practice; however, the trend was increasing in popularity with some of the students.

After a period of time, the situation came to a head. The father announced that as long as the son continued to have long hair, he would not be allowed to drive the family car.

The son replied, "Dad, that is not fair. A lot of men are wearing long hair. Even Jesus Christ had long hair."

The father said, "That's right, and he walked everywhere he went."

Case closed.

*I see that the flagpole still stands. Have your troops hoist the colors to its peak, and let no enemy ever take it down.*
– GENERAL DOUGLAS MACARTHUR

# THE LONG WAIT

Humor has always been a big part of my life. One of my favorite stories follows.

A man, Harry, and his wife, Janice, were sitting on their back porch, swinging in a porch swing. When Harry started crying softly, Janice said, "Harry, what is the matter with you? This should be the happiest day of your life. It is our fiftieth wedding anniversary. What is the problem?"

Harry said, "Do you remember when we were going together and your father found us in the back seat of my car making love?"

Janice said, "Yes, I remember."

Harry continued, "And he said if I didn't marry you, he would send me to jail for fifty years!"

Janice answered, "Yes."

Still crying, Harry said, "I would have gotten out today!"

*In 1998, one half million students dropped out of school in the United States.*
– UNKNOWN

# EXPOSED FROM A CAMPER

AFTER WORLD WAR II, CAMPERS BECAME POPULAR, especially with the retired people who had time to relax and travel on extended vacations.

We had a neighbor who had reached this point in life and was traveling far and wide. On one occasion, his wife was driving the pickup truck towing the camper. The husband, who had already driven for over one hundred miles that day, was relaxing in the camper. In fact, he had removed all his clothes with the exception of his undershorts.

The couple was in the process of driving through Fort Worth when the wife experienced some heavy road construction. On one occasion, it became exceedingly rough and finally caused a stop in all traffic. When this happened, the husband opened the back door of the camper and stepped out to see if they had been involved in a fender-bender accident.

This was not the case, and the wife immediately drove

on, unknowingly leaving her husband standing in the middle of the street with only his underwear on.

The husband quickly rushed to a service station and called a friend in Fort Worth. He explained the situation and asked him to take him home some twenty-two miles away. When they arrived at his house, he did not have a key, so they seated themselves on the porch waiting for the wife to arrive with the camper.

When the wife arrived, she was so surprised to see her husband on the porch and not in the camper that she became flustered and drove through the garage door before coming to a complete stop.

*Look for early warning signs of failure.*
– UNKNOWN

# TRAVELING INTERSTATE 10 BY FLASHLIGHT

ONE NIGHT WHEN I WAS RETURNING HOME FROM Houston following a speaking engagement, I noticed smoke coming from under the hood of my car. I pulled to the right side of the highway and stopped. I was hoping to determine the problem, but the engine died before I could tell what was causing the smoke. After a number of attempts to restart the engine, I gave up and called a wrecker service from a town about twenty miles away.

After about an hour, the wrecker arrived. Upon viewing the outward appearance of the wrecker, I wondered if I should not be the one providing roadside assistance to him, rather than him to me. After fifteen minutes, the necessary connections were made from the wrecker to the car, and we were on our way. We were going west on Interstate 10 and had gone perhaps ten miles when darkness set in. In about ten more miles, the wrecker lights dimmed and then went out completely.

The driver stopped, got out of the wrecker, and checked for the problem. When he returned to the driver's side, he fumbled around underneath the seat and pulled out a big five-battery flashlight, which he handed to me. I was instructed to hold it out my side of the window and to shine it on the white line on the right-hand side of the highway.

Without another word being spoken, we pulled back onto the interstate and headed west again. While I was holding the flashlight with the wind blowing in my face, I was very uncomfortable. As the miles went by, my arms grew tired, which caused the light to move off the white line. When this happened, the driver would very calmly remind me to keep the light on the white line. Every few miles, this dialogue would be repeated. Each time he had to remind me of my assignment, he increased the volume of his request.

As the miles passed, I found myself wondering, *Where is the highway patrol?* Here we were, on an interstate highway, with no lights on, while towing another car. The passing motorists would usually honk or change their lights from bright to low beam in an effort to let us know the lights were out. Finally, my skill of holding the light on the white line diminished to the extent that the driver yelled, "How do you expect me to keep the car on the road if you do not pay attention to shining the light on the white line?" I wanted to remind him that I was the paying customer and was not employed by the wrecker company. I refrained from doing so.

After driving 106 miles under these conditions, we finally arrived at my destination of Seguin, Texas. We left the interstate and proceeded to the garage in the downtown area. We had gone about five blocks when a Seguin police officer pulled us over. He asked about our problem. After our explanation, he offered to escort us to the garage of our choice. To my surprise, we were not issued a ticket!

Even though this was a memorable experience, I was happy to bid the wrecker driver good-bye.

*By 2020, more than 65 percent of jobs will demand training and education beyond high school.*
– UNKNOWN